THE RADICAL LUHMANN

THE RADI CAL LUH MANN

HANS-GEORG MOELLER

COLUMBIA UNIVERSITY PRESS
NEW YORK

Columbia University Press
Publishers Since 1893
New York   Chichester, West Sussex
cup.columbia.edu
Copyright © 2012 Columbia University Press

Library of Congress Cataloging-in-Publication Data
Moeller, Hans-Georg, 1964–
The Radical Luhmann / Hans-Georg Moeller
p. cm.
ISBN 978-0-231-15378-2 (cloth : alk. paper) — ISBN 978-0-231-15379-9
(pbk. : alk. paper) — ISBN 978-0-231-52717-0 (ebook)
1. Luhmann, Niklas, 1927–1998   2. Social systems—Philosophy.
3. Sociology—Philosophy. I. Title.
HM701.M635 2012
301.092—dc23

2011018977

∞

Columbia University Press books are printed on permanent
and durable acid-free paper.
This book is printed on paper with recycled content.
Printed in the United States of America

c 10 9 8 7 6 5 4 3 2 1
p 10 9 8 7 6 5 4 3 2 1

Book Design: Alejandro Largo

CONTENTS

PREFACE

It is striking that Niklas Luhmann's (1927–1998) social systems theory often provides the most advanced, adequate, and applicable models for understanding how things work in contemporary society. To give just one concrete example: in "Globalization or World Society? How to Conceive of Modern Society?" an article published in 1997, toward the end of his life, he not only answered these questions quite programmatically but also delineated in astonishing precision the economical developments that later led to the great financial crisis of 2008–2009.[1]

Luhmann did not *predict* the crisis as such, but he did succeed in giving an account of the social context that was to make it possible. And he could do so because his theoretical approach radically departs from mainstream political theory, which, according to him, has been mainly concerned with the utopian ideals of happiness and solidarity. Luhmann proclaims: "We have to come to terms, once and for all, with a society without human happiness and, of course, without taste, without solidarity, without similarity of living conditions. It makes no sense to insist on these aspirations, to revitalize or to supplement the list by renewing old names such as civil society or community." He appeals to social theorists to give up certain latent "idealist" and moralist pretensions: "Sociologists are not supposed to play the role of the lay-priests of modernity." According to Luhmann, the moralist tendency of a good deal of social and political thought is rooted in theoretical backwardness. The "lay-priests" of social theory still think of society in terms of the grand masters of the eighteenth and nineteenth centuries, namely in terms of stratification, that is, of a society divided into classes of oppressors and oppressed. He writes: "If we see stratification we will tend to see . . . injustice, exploitation and suppression; and we may wish to find corrective devices or at least to formulate normative schemes and moral injunctions that stimulate a rhetoric of critique and protest."[2] Luhmann advocates a radical departure from such a theoretical attitude. This is based on an acknowledgement that society has changed from stratified differentiation to functional differentiation. He declares: "If, on the other hand, we see functional differentiation, our description will point to the autonomy of the function systems, to their high degree of indifference, coupled to high sensitivity and irritability, in very specific respects that vary from system to system. Then, we will see a society without top and without centre; a society that evolves but cannot control itself."[3]

This change of perspective from that of the lay-priests to that of the radical theoretician is what I explore in this book. Or, in other words, I try to counter misinterpretations of Luhmann's theory, which, as Michael King said, failed to "recognize its radical nature and the paradigm that it introduces."[4] But let me first go back to how, in 1997, Luhmann outlined the social conditions of a financial crisis that occurred long after his death.

In a global society based on functional differentiation, "'international', indeed, no longer refers to a relation between two (or more) nations but to the political and the economic problems of the global system." In a radically deregionalized world society, "all internal boundaries depend upon the self-organization of subsystems and no longer on an 'origin' in history or on the nature or logic of the encompassing system." This leads to a situation in which "world society has reached a higher level of complexity with higher structural contingencies, more unexpected and unpredictable changes (some people call this 'chaos') and, above all, more interlinked dependencies and interdependencies. This means that causal constructions, (calculations, plannings) are no longer possible from a central and therefore 'objective' point of view."[5]

Within such a chaotically complex society, "there is no longer a quasi cosmological guarantee that structural developments within function systems remain compatible with each other." This means, for instance, that the "highly efficient modern medicine has demographic consequences"—that is "advances" in medicine lead to all kinds of social and economic problems, such as an imbalance in numbers between the old and the young and increasing health care costs. Similarly, the "new centrality of international financial markets, the corresponding marginalization of production, labour, and trade, and the transfer of economic security from real assets and first rate debtors to speculation itself, leads to a loss of jobs and seduces politicians to 'promise' jobs (without markets?)"—that is, the virtualization of the economy, the shift to an economy that focuses on financial products rather than goods creates immense wealth (for some) but undermines the traditional couplings of the economy with, for instance, infrastructure, means of production, labor, the legal system, and politics. In this way, society faces a novel "volatility of the financial market with its new derivative instruments for simultaneously maximizing security and risk with unpredictable effects." In other words: "The economic system has shifted its bases of security from property and reliable debtors (such as states or large corporations) to speculation itself. He who tries to maintain his property will lose his fortune, and he who tries to maintain and increase his wealth will have to change his investments one day to the next. He can either use new derivative instruments or must trust some of the many funds that do this for him."[6] For Luhmann, all this cannot be explained on the basis of the traditional vocabulary of "exploitation" or with moralist categories such as "greed."

The developments in the financial sector of the economy and the nearly catastrophic effects of these developments—on the education system in Ireland, for instance —quite clearly demonstrate that Luhmann was right when he said: "we are not in a phase of '*posthistoire*' but, on the contrary, in a phase of turbulent evolution without predictable outcome."[7] In this situation, sticking to the vocabulary of political theory that has been developed by the philosophers of the past three or four centuries does not seem to be a promising strategy. Luhmann says: "At present, the unsolved problems surrounding the concept of society seem to prevent theoretical progress. The idea of a good, or, at least, a better society still dominates the field. Sociologists, interested in theory, continue to explore the old mazes with diminishing returns instead of moving into new ones. It might be rewarding, however, not to look for better solutions of problems—of problems that are constructed by the mass media—but to ask 'what is the problem?' in the first place."[8]

So, what is the problem? And, moreover, how do we have to change our point of view so that we are better able to see it? The following chapters explore Luhmann's paradigm shift from philosophy to theory that opens up new perspectives on the contemporary world.

I begin my exposition with an attempt to characterize the very social system within which Luhmann's writings were produced, that is the German academic "scene" of the last decades of the twentieth century. Within this social environment, Luhmann was able to succeed despite, or perhaps because of, the challenges he posed to Habermas's dominating doctrine of a society based on "domination-free discourse" (*herrschaftsfreier Diskurs*). Luhmann offered a radical alternative to this normative political philosophy. He conceived of his theory as a subversive Trojan horse that, once inside the enemy's camp, might destroy them from within. I argue that one of the tactics employed by Luhmann to disguise this threat was his often rather convoluted writing style. By adopting the jargon of Habermas and others who constituted the academic elite of the time, Luhmann was granted entry into their Troy.

After these preliminary considerations, I move on to look at various aspects of what I believe to be a shift from philosophy to theory in Luhmann's works. Luhmann breaks with the anthropocentric heritage of modern Western philosophy. More so than any other of the humanities, philosophy has been looking to humans as "the measure of all things," particularly in political and social philosophy. Luhmann's "fourth insult" to human vanity consists in denying the notion of the "human being" a central place in social theory. He follows earlier non-anthropocentric shifts that occurred in cosmology (Copernicus), biology (Darwin), and psychology (Freud). Unsurprisingly, this insult, just as with its historical predecessors, has been perceived by many as scandalous and continues to make Luhmann a persona non grata in some ideological camps.

Chapter 4, "From Necessity to Contingency," deals with a comparison between Luhmann and Hegel. In my view, Hegel is the most important philosophical influence on Luhmann. However, the relation between the two great systemic thinkers is rather ambiguous. I argue that Luhmann attempted a Hegelian *Aufhebung* (sublation) of Hegel's philosophy. Just as Hegel tried to sublate religion through philosophy (in the threefold sense of lifting it to a higher level, overcoming it, and preserving it), Luhmann intended to sublate philosophy through theory. For Hegel, the task of philosophy consisted in transforming contingency into necessity. Luhmann's theory aims to transform necessity into contingency.

In chapter 5, "The Last Footnote to Plato," I outline what I believe to be the most obvious, and yet most overlooked, achievement of the Luhmannian shift to theory: a solution to a central problem of traditional Western philosophy, mind-body dualism. After Descartes, and in negative reaction to him, attempts to deal with his strong dualism typically aimed at reconciling the body and the mind in such a way as to emancipate the body. The preoccupation with the mind-body discourse led to an incapability to think "outside the box" and to develop more radical alternatives to this dualism. Luhmann convincingly shows that there is at least one more dimension in addition to the intellectual and the physical, namely communication. This third dimension allowed Luhmann to replace traditional substance dualism with a functional theory of structural couplings between different systemic realms.

In chapter six, I discuss Luhmann's "metabiological" approach (to use a term coined by Habermas) to social theory, which marks another break with mainstream modern social and political thought. Enlightenment and post-Enlightenment philosophy tended to look at civil society and the individuals who were believed to constitute it in terms of autonomous agency. Free will, rationality, and responsibility allow humans to shape society and to emerge from their "self-inflicted immaturity." In this way, humans become self-creators. They are the ultimate masters of their fate and the society in which they live. From an evolutionary perspective, however, such self-steering or self-governing is an illusion. From the perspective of systems theory, the social world, just as nature, consists of many complex system-environment relations that have no room or use for any intelligent designer or autonomous governor.

In chapter 7, "Constructivism as Postmodernist Realism," I discuss Luhmann's self-identification as a "radical constructivist." I point out that constructivism and realism are not inherently contradictory—specifically not in Luhmann's case. Luhmann's constructivism is a cognitive constructivism, that is, it is epistemological. Cognitive construction is the "condition of the possibility" for the emergence of reality; it distinguishes that which is from that which is not, and thereby realizes the real. In this way, cognitive construction radicalizes German idealism and reverses the relation between ontology and epistemology. For Luhmann, reality is not the a priori condition for experience. Instead, he argues that cognitive functions are capable of generating themselves "autopoietically" and thereby of constructing reality—and that they can do so in multiple ways. Reality, as an effect of cognitive self-generation and construction, is not based on identity, but on difference, and this makes it no less real.

My analysis of Luhmann's understanding of democracy in chapter 8 examines the limitations of social steering in a more concrete way. Luhmann puts into question the very notion of democratic participation. According to him, the idea of democracy as rule of the people is no more than a utopian fantasy. It fails to meaningfully describe the functioning of politics in contemporary society. Rather than reflecting on how society may be able to become more democratic and to ultimately allow the people to rule themselves, Luhmann suggests a functionalist concept of democracy as a symbolic narrative that allows the political system to construct legitimacy. Paradoxically, attempts to make society more democratic may in fact endanger the functioning of democratic politics. Luhmann's political radicalism is therefore not an ideological radicalism but an anti-ideological one.

The conclusion attempts to answer what is perhaps an inappropriate question: where does Luhmann's radicalism ultimately lead us? Or, how can a Luhmannian attitude toward society, and, indeed, life, be described? I suggest that this attitude can be defined as a cultivation of modesty, irony, and equanimity.

The appendix contains a short overview of Luhmann's life and his theory.

I thank Anne R. Gibbons, Andrew Whitehead, and Jason Dockstader very much for correcting my English and for suggesting many changes and improvements. I am indebted to Bruce Clarke, Michael King, and

Elena Esposito for their detailed comments and criticisms of drafts of this book. I am grateful to Wendy Lochner at Columbia University Press for taking on this "radical" project. I appreciate the support for this publication given by the College of Arts, Celtic Studies and Social Sciences, University College Cork, Ireland.

IN
TRO
DUC
TION

ONE

THE TROJAN HORSE
LUHMANN'S (NOT SO) HIDDEN RADICALISM

If, as I think, Luhmann's social theory is the best description and analysis of contemporary society presently available, then it is only fair to ask why the majority of people—not only in the wider public, but also in academic circles—have apparently failed to notice this, and why Luhmann's name remains far less prominent and less well known than that of Hobbes or Marx, or Foucault or Habermas.[1]

The first and most immediate reason for Luhmann's relative obscurity, particularly in North America, may well be found in what I describe in the following section, namely his often "soporific" style.[2] While the somewhat off-putting effect of Luhmann's texts on some North American readers is quite coincidental—since, after all, Luhmann wrote in German and for a German language audience—he might well have been aware of a certain advantage brought about by his esoteric writings in his home country. This style fit well with the contemporary sociological discourse of which he was a part. At home, his perfectly common German university idiom gained him, on the one hand, the respect of those who did not understand him, and, on the other hand, made him appear unsuspicious to his peers. This enabled him, I believe, to actually say a lot of things that he could not have said otherwise without risking being thoroughly ostracized by the post-1968 German academic community. Luhmann's theory contained so many radicalisms that he needed to conceal them within the awkward Trojan horse of a largely unassuming and inaccessible language. The American "liberal orthodoxy" might dismiss or simply ignore Luhmann—this was not a concern for him, as he was a German university professor—but he had to ensure that he did not too openly shock the ideologically extremely cautious (after the Nazi disaster) academic community in his immediate environment. Therefore, I believe, he might well have consciously cultivated his murkiness in order to conceal certain potentially inflammatory aspects of his theory from the eyes of those who were still too weak (in a Nietzschean sense) to look at them plainly.

This book is primarily aimed at bringing these radical aspects of Luhmann's theory to the fore. As far as I can tell, Luhmann was rather successful at hiding the issues that I am going to address. The reception of his theory has generally focused on less explosive aspects of his work. While he has been labeled a conservative theoretician, he has seldom been called a radical. This book is an attempt to justify such a label.

Interestingly enough, Luhmann's radicalism is not *that* hidden. In fact, once one becomes aware of this radicalism, one finds explicit references to it throughout his work. He rather frequently uses the term radical to characterize his positions. These references are typically hidden within his convoluted prose, but, nevertheless, stick out rather conspicuously if one is attentive.

In an interview toward the end of his life, Luhmann stated: "It had always been clear to me that a thoroughly constructed conceptual theory of society would be much more radical and much more discomforting in its effects than narrowly focused criticisms—criticisms of capitalism for instance—could ever imagine."[3] This is a remarkable pronouncement. Not only does Luhmann openly declare his radical intentions, but he explicitly says that he intended his theory to be "much more radical and discomforting"—that is, more revolutionary—than, well, Marxism. This somewhat surprising admission of a so-called conservative thinker is reiterated in another interview published in the same volume. There, Luhmann ascribes to his theory the "political effect of a Trojan horse."[4] This image illustrates both the *se-*

crecy and *de(con)structive intent* of Luhmann's radicalism. Luhmann openly admits to his attempt to smuggle into social theory, hidden in his writings, certain contents that could demolish and replace dominating self-descriptions, not only of social theory itself, but of society at large. This is quite a fiery claim, one that I explore and clarify further on the following pages.

In the section "From Philosophy to Theory," I trace various ways in which Luhmann has radically departed from the traditional old-European theoretical heritage. This departure is in many ways so radical that the term "philosophy" was not appropriate for what he was intending—namely supertheory. For Luhmann, philosophy had lost its capacity to lend expression to what, in post-Hegelian times, could be called a convincing self-description of contemporary society. For Luhmann the concepts, the basic vocabulary, and even the foundational questions of philosophy had become largely obsolete. He wanted to sublate the entire enterprise into something new: radical theory.[5]

One of Luhmann's most provocative self-designations was "radical antihumanist." This, of course, was not an indication of sympathy for satanically inhumane values, methods, or political programs, but an attempt to fundamentally "de-anthropologize" the description of society and of the world in general. This already constitutes a major break with the Western philosophical tradition, which had been thoroughly humanist. Even for modern philosophers such as Heidegger, human beings were still considered the caretakers of Being, and even highly technical analytic philosophy and philosophy of mind are still basically concerned with the analysis of human language and consciousness. In accordance with this unchallenged anthropocentric dogma of Western philosophy from Plato up to and including the twentieth century, philosophy had always included ethical deliberations and pronouncements. The world was considered in an anthropocentric fashion not only with respect to what was considered knowable but also with respect to what was envisioned as doable. Therefore, anthropocentric philosophy generally entailed pronouncements about how to behave—either as individuals or as a collective. Luhmann's "radical antihumanism" is not limited to a redescription of reality in a nonanthropocentric way. It includes a dismissal of human agency. Theory, as opposed to philosophy, no longer tries to outline the doable, but rather to explain why the very notion of "doability" or "action" has become rather problematic. A radically antihumanist theory tries to explain why anthropocentrism—having been abolished in cosmology, biology, and psychology—now has to be abolished in social theory. Once this abolition has taken place, there is not much room left for traditional philosophical enquiries of a humanistic sort.

One way to illustrate the rift between Luhmann's theory and traditional philosophy is by comparing him to Hegel, one of the last grand systemic thinkers in the history of philosophy. While Luhmann probably shared the monumental aspirations of authors such as Hegel, his theory entails an ironical reflection on its own limitations. Systemic philosophy has been traditionally concerned with establishing veritable truths, that is, not mere dogmas. What was outlined as being true had to be proven to be so. For Descartes, for instance, everything depended not on truth, but on the *certainty* of the true. In Hegel's works, the Cartesian notion of certainty was replaced by reflections on the *necessity* of whatever was true or real. In this way, systematic philosophy commonly included some sort of inner mechanism that would serve to anchor its propositions and conclusions in something more fundamental than the system itself; this is commonly called "foundationalism." Luhmann's shift from philosophy to theory, however, is about denouncing such anchoring strategies. Systematic theory, as opposed to traditional systematic philosophy, is antifoundationalist; it does not attempt to prove its necessity, but to explain its own contingency. In this way, unlike "serious" philosophy, theory implies an ironical attitude toward itself, that is, it admits to some sort of *Münchhausen* effect, a trick by which it is able to pull itself out of the mud by its own hair.

Another radical aspect of Luhmann's theory is what may be called its Alexandrian solution of the Gordian knot of the age-old mind-body problem. Rather than trying to reunite these two notions as a consequence of a post-Platonic, post-Christian, and post-Cartesian nostalgia for the reunion of the physical and the spiritual, Luhmann explains why this traditional dualism has never been pluralistic enough. He finds that one other dimension of reality has been obscured by the mind-body dualism, namely, communication. In this way, rather than following the philosophical trend of attempting to heal the Cartesian split, Luhmann adds at least one more differentiation. Interestingly enough, this switch from dualism to triadism, or pluralism, also offers a solution to the traditional mechanical problem of the connection between mind and body that allows them to influence one another. Luhmann's theory of operationally closed systems is, at the same time, also a second-order cybernetic theory of nontrivial or complex systems, which, being in a system-environment relation, are open for mutual resonance, perturbation, and irritation. Given Luhmann's emphasis on the "operational closure" of systems, including the operational closure of bodily and mental systems, the fact that this closure is the very condition for their *openness* to mutual influence has sometimes been neglected. In other words, operational closure *results in* cognitive openness. Luhmann stated very explicitly: "The concept of a self-referentially closed system does not contradict the system's *openness to the environment.*"[6]

The openness of systems to one another stipulates their openness to their environment—since the environment of a system includes other systems. Therefore, Luhmann's theory also represents a radical *ecologism.* Systems theory is systems-environment theory, and therefore an ecological theory. In the Darwinian tradition, and following the post-Darwinian evolutionary biologists Humberto Maturana and Francisco Varela, a theory of ecosystems is at the same time a theory of evolution. Transferring ecological evolutionary theory from biology to sociology, Luhmann challenges traditional "creationist" points of view, which, in a secularized form, still dominate mainstream conceptions of society. While evolutionary ecology is no longer perceived as scandalous by most natural scientists, it can be very provocative when applied in the rather anthropocentric areas of social sciences or "*human*ities." Luhmann's radical ecological approach to society minimizes the possibilities for steering social developments or history. In the same way that a species cannot biologically control, or even adequately project, its future—because of its intricate entanglement in highly complex coevolutionary processes that go on simultaneously between systems and their environments—Luhmann proposes that social systems (especially human agents) cannot control social developments. Luhmann's ecological evolution theory means that society has no center, just as an ecosystem has no center. Therefore society has never been (and will never be) open for creationist interventions by divine or secular sources.

Ecological evolutionary theory, as opposed to creationist views, easily leads to the radical constructivism that Luhmann ascribes to himself. Just as biological evolution is a constructivist self-generation of life, society is an effect of social reality construction through communication. Constructivism and relativism are therefore not antagonistic. To the contrary, they can imply one another, as is the case with Luhmann's social systems theory. Social reality is an effect of contingent autopoietic or self-generative processes, but this does not diminish the extent of its reality. Traditional social theorists may say that declaring such social values as justice, freedom, or human dignity as "mere" social constructs somehow devalues them ontologically. For Luhmann, however, constructivism, including social constructivism, is not merely an epistemology—it not only explains how cognition works—but also an ontology: it explains how reality is produced. Therefore, from the perspective of radical constructivism, the reality of social constructs can be considered even more solid than the supposed reality of what may be called transcendent or transcendental illusions. In this way, Luhmann's radical constructivism entails a postmodernist ontology that acknowledges and affirms the contingent and plural as being fully real and not, in any way, ontologically deficient.

Following this outline of what I consider to be the most radical and explosive aspects within Luhmann's theory, I turn to a more concrete discussion of a provocative "deconstruction" that follows from the theory's basic assertions. I look at how Luhmann critically dissects one central contemporary "narrative" (to use another postmodernist term), the discourse of democracy. This discourse is still generally believed to be more than merely a discourse. It is thought to be a substantial description of the foundations and normative aspirations of our society. Luhmann tackles this idea, which is very much at the core of contemporary "civil religion." Society, instead of being democratic in any politically or socially meaningful sense, applies the utopian rhetorics of democracy as a set of semantic blinders that allows it to do whatever it does *smoothly,* that is, without having to observe potentially irritating alternatives—at least until the arrival of the Trojan horse of social systems theory.

TWO

WHY HE WROTE SUCH BAD BOOKS

On Amazon.com, a reader of my book *Luhmann Explained* wrote: "Niklas Luhmann was a student of Talcott Parsons, from whom he apparently learned only how to write impossibly vague and convoluted prose. I have found reading Luhmann extremely soporific, so I thought perhaps this book [*Luhmann Explained*] might be refreshingly lucid and penetrating. Perhaps, I thought, if I could only stay awake, I could learn a lot from Luhmann. Alas, such does not appear to be the case." The review concludes with some practical advice: "If your teenager is bad, don't ground him; make him write an essay on the sociological theory of Niklas Luhmann."[1]

I sympathize with this reader's views. Having read texts by Luhmann for about twenty years, I have increasingly asked myself why, even though I find the theory very appealing, its inventor did not manage to express it in a reasonably enjoyable manner. Sometimes, particularly in his later works, Luhmann's irony and humor interrupt his otherwise extremely dry, unnecessarily convoluted, poorly structured, highly repetitive, overly long, and aesthetically unpleasing texts. The irony and humor are refreshing, but do not suffice to rescue most of his books and many of his articles from being, generally speaking, "extremely soporific" reading material. I readily admit, the material sometimes made me fall asleep.

I have been able to come up with several explanations as to why

Luhmann was such a bad writer—at least in comparison with, in my view, the brilliance of his theory. All of these reasons, I stress, are explanations, not excuses.

The inherent reason for Luhmann's bad writing is the peculiar way in which he actually produced his texts. Luhmann's published oeuvre is enormous. Not only are his books exceptionally numerous, they are also usually very long, often exceeding five hundred pages. Luhmann's prolificacy was quite methodical. He not only spent most of his time writing,[2] but also developed a sort of mechanics of production by making use of a huge note cabinet (*Zettelkasten*) that he had been assembling throughout his life. He made short notes of ideas, thoughts, quotations, and references to the literature he read. Then he arranged these notes according to a self-developed numerical ordering system that included "links" from one note to others. He could thereby trace his way through the notes in various ways. He spent more time organizing and composing the note cabinet than writing actual texts. The books and articles had only to be extracted from the cabinet. Luhmann said: "I first make a plan of what I am going to write, and then take from the note cabinet what I can use."[3]

One effect of this way of writing was, as Luhmann himself admitted, the lack of a clear narrative development. He stated: "I can move from any number to any other number in the note cabinet. Thus, there is no linearity, but a spider-like system that can be started anywhere." And he added: "This technique, I believe, explains why I do not at all think in a linear way, and why I have trouble finding the right chapter sequence when writing books, since, properly, any chapter should reappear in any of the others."[4]

The nonlinearity of Luhmann's texts makes them not reader-friendly. On the one hand, materials reappear a lot throughout his writings. Even short papers on specific topics typically include passages about Luhmann's general theory that are hardly comprehensible for the uninitiated reader. In most of his works, Luhmann presents the reader with an assemblage of new remarks about a particular issue along with lengthy repetitions of information about his theoretical framework. While Luhmann was right in stating that a reader can start more or less anywhere in his books, it is also true that one cannot really *begin*

anywhere.[5] There is no beginning or gradual initiation to his books—
and far less so with regard to the whole theoretical project. Reading
Luhmann is therefore frustrating at the beginning, given that the
reader is confronted with unknown and unexplained terminology and
slightly chaotic shifts between ideas, remarks, and themes. It takes a
lot of practice before one can understand how Luhmann uses his idiosyncratic theoretical terminology (which appears to be incoherent
at first, since it is borrowed in part from a number of highly diverse
sources). And even after one has gained a basic understanding of this
terminology, one's initial frustrating experience is only replaced with
another one, namely that of tiring repetitions and interruptions in
Luhmann's often all too lengthy writings.

A second factor contributing to the forbidding nature of Luhmann's
style is what could be called the intellectual heritage that he chose to
continue. Luhmann explicitly aimed at constructing a "supertheory."[6]
He was therefore willing to connect with the ambitions of the grand
theoretical systems of eighteenth- and nineteenth-century German
idealism and, in particular, its two main representatives, Kant and
Hegel. Not only are these two philosophers often referred to in his
writings, but it is quite obvious that Luhmann followed them in trying
to develop a novel scientific system, which, by being a new theoretical
conceptual terminology, had to be sufficiently technical and abstract
in order to be applied to an analysis of, basically, *anything*. On the one
hand, this meant the creation of an idiosyncratic vocabulary in the
sense of crucial expressions and words that were either neologisms or
used outside of their normal meaning. On the other hand, it also led
to the vagueness criticized by the aforementioned Amazon.com reviewer, namely, a lack of concrete definitions for the core terminology.

One of the lecturers who introduced Hegel during my first semes-
ters at university frequently had to respond to complaints by students
about the unintelligibility of the Hegelian terms. Students often said
that they did not know how to mentally represent (*vorstellen*) the
meaning of these words—they did not know what to concretely think
of when Hegel wrote in his conceptual manner. The lecturer would
explain that Hegel's intent was to prevent his readers from having any
concrete mental representations. Concepts or ideas are meant to be

purely conceptual—just as one begins to think mathematically when one no longer has to imagine, let's say, three fingers or three apples when the number three is mentioned, but understands the concept of three as such without recourse to a concrete image. Even though Luhmann is not an idealist, the terminology of his supertheory often, out of necessity, escapes concrete definitions. Terms such as "distinction" or "observation" are extremely formal. They can be applied in the analysis of nearly limitless concrete (social) phenomena, but cannot be *concretely* defined—only *formally* (and this with equally formal terminology).

Luhmann not only inherited the formality of his conceptual vocabulary from philosophers like Hegel and Kant, but also their monumental approach. For these thinkers, a scientific supertheory had to be "supersized." None of them considered brevity a virtue. In order to be considered serious, a scientific philosophical system of their time had to be large. Such projects as a "phenomenology of the spirit" or a "critique of pure reason" were so encompassing that they simply had to materially consist of hundreds of pages. One could also write shorter, more "popular" treatises (such as Kant's *Prolegomena to any Future Metaphysics* was supposed to be), but the system itself had to impress through its sheer volume. I think that since Luhmann saw himself as continuing the heritage of "supertheoreticians" like Kant and Hegel (or Marx or Weber in social theory), he also aspired to produce an oeuvre that, in a library, would look at first sight just as impressive as theirs.

It was not only mere quantity, of course, that constituted the heaviness of the systems of the traditional supertheorists, but also their difficulty. Science (in the sense of the German term *Wissenschaft,* which encompasses all academic disciplines including natural sciences, social sciences, and the humanities) had to be esoteric, not "straightforward." Again, this may be explained by an anecdote from German academic philosophy. A friend of mine, Günter Wohlfart, himself a former German philosophy professor, obtained his Ph.D. in the late 1960s and early 1970s in Frankfurt under the supervision of Adorno and Habermas. Günter once missed a presentation by a visiting lecturer and later asked another student who had been there if it had been any good. The student replied enthusiastically and in all seriousness: "It was awesome—I did not understand a word!" The greatness of a philosophical, scientific, and theoretical book was, within the science and education systems in Germany, measured by, among other indicators, its inaccessibility. The time and mental effort that one had to invest in order to understand a philosophical or theoretical book was considered to be an effect of the quality of the work itself. The more difficult it was to penetrate, the more penetrating the author was supposed to be.

Luhmann was perhaps aware of the difference between German (as well as Continental European as a whole) and North American attitudes toward academic, and, in particular, philosophical and theoretical literature. It may be for this reason that he, somewhat apologetically, though no doubt proudly, and perhaps even somewhat conceitedly, began his preface to the English translation of *Social Systems* (published in the United States by Stanford University Press) by stating: "This is not an easy book. It does not accommodate those who prefer a quick and easy read, yet do not want to die without a taste of systems theory."[7] In North America, writers and lecturers, including those in an academic setting, are normally assumed to attempt to make themselves understood to their audience. This is considered reputable. In Germany, however, at least since the times of Kant and Hegel, academic audiences are supposed to appreciate the uncompromising intellectual rigidity of a professor who demonstrates his (or, nowadays, also her) competence by not making any attempt to satisfy populist demands. In fact, in an academic context, speakers and writers might well demand that the audience prove itself worthy of the ones addressing it-- just as Luhmann did in his preface to *Social Systems.*

A third reason for Luhmann's unappealing and, from my perspective, often clumsy writing style is closely related to the second, namely the German academic discourse and intellectual heritage of which he was a part. In other words, Luhmann (or rather, his writing) suffered from being too closely associated with the German academic elite at the time. Other great philosophical or theoretical writers were lucky enough to enjoy a certain distance from the German language academia and were therefore much less (if at all) infected by the disease of bad writing that had plagued it for a long time. I think of such authors as Marx, Nietzsche, and Wittgenstein. Unlike those men, Luhmann wrote his texts in an environment of academically pretentious and soporific authors equal to those of his theoretical nemesis Jürgen Habermas.

The widespread cultural revolution of the late 1960s took on a very specific shape in Germany. It was a highly theoretical affair—more so, I believe, than, for instance, in the United States (with the civil rights movement, draft dodging, etc.) or Italy (with its workers' strikes) where much more practical issues were at stake. In Germany, the revolution was largely academic, and the language used by the academic revolutionaries on the left was just as grotesquely elitist as that of the traditional elites against whom they were revolting. The "progressive" academic authors in Germany were certainly not a stylistic avant-garde. Perhaps one of the reasons that, despite the huge ideological and theoretical disparities between Luhmann and leftist social thinkers like Habermas, a dialogue between the two sides was actually *possible*, was that they shared a *jargon* (to borrow Adorno's famous expression). This jargon has been uniting the German academic world, as far as I can tell, until today—and, at the same time, has served to isolate it from the rest of the world. It would have been nice if Luhmann had somehow been able to escape from it, but, "alas, such does not appear to be the case."

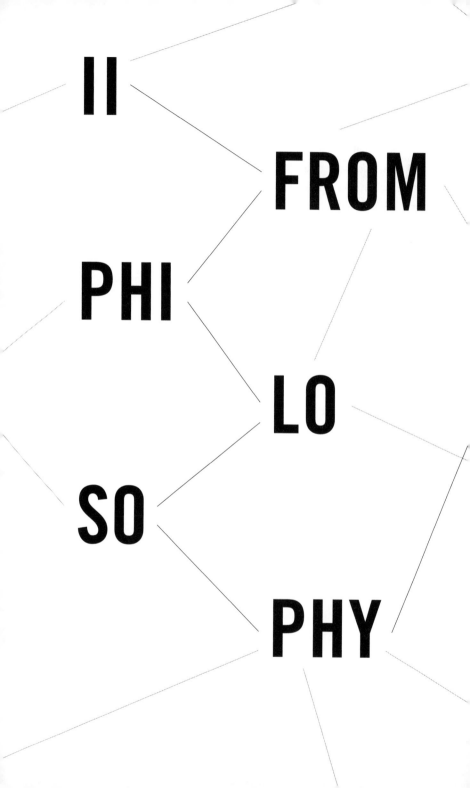

II

FROM

PHI

LO

SO

PHY

THREE

THE FOURTH INSULT
A REFUTATION OF HUMANISM

In the first chapter of his later magnum opus *Die Gesellschaft der Gesellschaft* (The Society of Society), Niklas Luhmann candidly declares, in a highly programmatic and uncompromising way, that his theory is to be understood as an attempt at a "transition towards a radically anti-humanist, a radically anti-regionalist, and a radically constructivist concept of society." He flatly denies the common assumption "that a society consists of concrete human beings and relations between human beings."[1] Such a rhetorically conspicuous and unhidden declaration of the radicalism of his antihumanist intentions is quite unusual for Luhmann, at least in his earlier works. It seems that in his last major work—probably already aware of his fatal illness, Luhmann must have considered that this was his last chance to present his theory in a general and summarizing fashion—he wanted to depart, at least on this occasion, from his trademark obscurity, hidden irony, and sarcasm, and intended to position himself as straightforwardly as possible so as not to be misunderstood.

Luhmann's antihumanism positions him in direct contradiction to common sense and mainstream political thought and makes it rather difficult to "propagate" his version of social systems theory, particularly in North America. More so than in any other region, the discourse in North America, both academic and political—and even the public discourse of the mass media—still relies heavily on the semantics of the "old-European" Enlightenment tradition of the eighteenth century. It often seems to me that the American Revolution has not yet really ended. A similar observation was made by the Italian sociologist Danilo Zolo. Zolo advocates a "realist" theory of contemporary democracy and explicitly distances himself from the "fruitless (and inevitably moralistic) resurrection of the ethico-political prescription of classical democracy in the old European tradition" as represented by a number of Anglo-American authors such as John Rawls. He states very pointedly that those prescriptions "add up to little more in substance than a harking back to the puritan individualism of European proto-Capitalism, whose political ideals, it has been said, extended no further than the intellectual horizon of the eighteenth-century ironmonger."[2]

I believe Zolo's point can be nicely illustrated by simply looking at what is perhaps the most often cited representative phrase of American revolutionary thought, namely the famous words of the Declaration of Independence: "We hold these truths to be self-evident: that all men are created equal; that they are endowed by their Creator with inherent and unalienable rights; that among these are life, liberty, and the pursuit of happiness; that to secure these rights, governments are instituted among men, deriving their just powers from the consent of the governed."[3] These words programmatically express the optimistic political humanism of the Enlightenment. They ascribe, based on a supposed divine creation, specific rights, qualities, and goals that were perceived to be "self-evident" in the sociocultural context of "the puritan individualism of European proto-Capitalism," to humans in general and posits them at the center of a social and political agenda. These half divine, half human rights, qualities, and goals are still widely revered, publicly and privately, both in the United States and in the Western world more generally, and it is believed that, while they are not fully realized, they are still among the most important ideals informing any civilized society. From a Luhmannian perspective, however, nothing in the quotation from the Declaration of Independence is of any theoretical value for explaining how present-day society (and, I think, particularly North American society) actually operates.

I think it makes no sense to present a "Luhmann lite" and to understand him as a representative of a "weak posthumanism" that would somehow try to preserve some humanist values while going beyond humanism as such. He labeled himself differently and took himself as a radical *anti*humanist, and it has to be expected that this radicalism will not be very palatable to many readers, particularly not in a culture like North America that holds on so dearly to the concept of a civil society.

Luhmann did not conceive of social systems theory, to put it in McLuhan's terms, as a theory that deals with the "extensions of man." He did not aim at a new understanding of what it means to be human in the wake of a technological revolution. Luhmann can be considered a "strong posthumanist"[4] (unlike McLuhan and his followers) insofar as he does not suppose that society has somehow stretched itself beyond its human limitations. Instead, he thinks that the value of conceiving of society in human and subject-centered terms has become limited. Luhmann does not discuss the modifications of *being human* in a technological age; rather, he discusses the *social modifications* that went along with technological change. He characterizes himself as a radical antihumanist because he thinks that the humanist self-description of society has been fundamentally flawed from the start. The world has never been human, and thus there has never been a shift from a human to a posthuman world.

According to Luhmann, we do not live in a postmodern world. Modernity, as the period of functional differentiation, is still ongoing. The recent technological changes are, theoretically speaking, external to society. Like human bodies and minds, technology is not a part of society, but belongs to the environment of the social system.[5] Neither humans nor computers communicate, only communication does. This is not to deny the profound social influences of recent technological developments (which have been successfully traced, for instance, by N. Katherine Hayles and Donna J. Haraway), but to treat them strictly as external influences on society. Society, according to Luhmann, was never human—the notion of the "human being" has always been theoretically problematic, and a sociology based on humanist terms has always been misguided.

In his critical—and seminal—essay on Luhmann in *The Philosophical Discourse of Modernity*, Jürgen Habermas calls Luhmann's theory "metabiological." Habermas defines this term in the following way: "However the expression 'metaphysics' may have chanced to arise, one could attribute to it the meaning of a thinking that proceeds from the 'for us' of physical appearances and asks what lies behind them. Then we can use the term 'metabiological' for a thinking that starts from the 'for itself' of organic life and goes behind it—the cybernetically described, basic phenomenon of the self-maintenance of self-relating systems in the face of hypercomplex environments."[6]

Contemporary systems theory is concerned in general with the "for itself" of systems, with self-generating and self-reproducing (i.e., autopoietic) entities. These entities construct themselves within an environment by differentiating themselves from this environment. As Habermas correctly stresses, the paradigmatic example of such autopoietic systems are biological systems (such as cells, immune systems, etc.). An autopoietic system that is "for itself" consists of the operations that constitute the self-reproduction of the system. Biological systems consist of their internal biological processes. Analogously, psychic systems (i.e., minds) consist of internal psychological operations (such as thoughts and feelings). Brains are biological systems, and minds are psychic systems. Brainwaves are continued with further brainwaves, not with thoughts. Similarly, thoughts have to be continued with more thoughts, not with brainwaves. The brain and the mind are systemically separated. They cannot mutually interfere with one another's operations; they are environments for one another. Similarly, communication cannot be continued with either thoughts or brainwaves. Neither minds nor brains can speak. We have developed the linguistic habit of confusing these three empirically distinct systemic realms.[7]

If we want to understand how the brain works, we have to describe physiological and biological processes, not thoughts and social phenomena, which, while they may well influence these processes as environmental factors, remain operationally distinct from them. Analogously, if we want to describe how the mind works, we have to focus on psychological processes. If we want to describe society, we have to focus on communicative processes. It is not helpful scientifically to say that human brainwaves are primarily human rather than cerebral. If we want to be scientifically precise, we have to say that human brainwaves are a phenomenon of brain activity and not of human activity. In the same way, we have to say that feelings are a phenomenon of psychic activity, and that communications (such as, for instance, this written document) are phenomena of communicational or social activity. Social systems theory is "metabiological" in the sense that it looks at society as a complex assembly of communication systems, just as bodies are complex assemblies of biological systems. The emphasis is, in both cases, on the operational for-selfness of the systems. To say that humans are "brain-active," think, and communicate is not wrong, but imprecise. None of these activities are exclusively or essentially human.

Luhmann famously (or infamously) claims that humans cannot communicate, instead only communication systems can: "Within the communication system we call society, it is conventional to assume that humans can communicate. Even clever analysts have been fooled by this convention. It is relatively easy to see that this statement is false and that it only functions as a convention and only within communication. The convention is necessary because communication necessarily addresses its operations to those who are required to continue communication. Humans cannot communicate; not even their brains can communicate; not even their conscious minds can communicate. Only communication can communicate."[8] This statement, in my view, is meant "metabiologically," that is, it is analogous to the statement that humans cannot produce brainwaves, only brains can. It does not deny the existence of human beings, but says that humans are as little in control of social functions as they are of brain functions. In other words, it aims at making sociology as little (or as much) humanist as brain physiology in order to allow for a more adequate terminology and thus a better theory of social mechanisms.

As human beings, we have a biological body, a mental mind, and are addressed as persons in communication. However, there is no discernable systemic unit that could successfully combine these three operationally differentiated realms. Society is a system in which, following the biological metaphor, communicational organisms emerge and are able to maintain themselves in symbiosis with biological and psychic systems. In a functionally differentiated society, these communicational organisms are the different social function systems. Sociology can observe and describe how these systems function, what structures they develop, which codes they apply, how they are coupled with other systems, and so on. Within society, the human being is merely an all too convenient traditional notion, a communicational tool that remains obscure and confused. Just as in science we call people who do biological research on humans biologists, and not humanists, we also acknowledge that people who do research on society are sociologists rather than humanists. In the end, Luhmann's radical antihumanism does not amount to much more than a theoretical confirmation of this perfectly common academic self-designation.

This outline of Luhmann's "dis-humanization" of sociology has far-reaching consequences when it comes to an analysis of the dominating humanist self-descriptions within society. Here, I look briefly at one aspect of Luhmann's theory that rather clearly shows that Luhmann rigorously departs from humanist social theories and aims at deconstructing commonsense humanist notions of how our society works. This aspect is Luhmann's conception of politics.[9]

The dominant semantics of both public discourse and social theory assume that humans can somehow intervene in society and, in some instances, even steer it. After all, we have a specific social system that is supposed to fulfill this role, namely the political system. The government is meant to steer society—like a captain steers the ship (to refer back to the ancient Greek root of the verb "to govern"). Luhmann, however maintains: "Although all steering takes place within society and therefore always executes the autopoiesis of society (i.e., communicates) there is, in the strict sense of the word, no self-steering of society on the level of the entire system." Under the conditions of functional differentiation and operational closure, there is no institution, organization, system, or group in society that can steer society as a whole. Systems steer themselves, and the political system can, strictly speaking, only steer itself. It can "irritate" or "perturb" other systems, but it has no immediate causal power over other systems. Luhmann categorically states: "Steering is always self-steering of systems."[10]

There is no central steering agency in a society that is constituted by a multiplicity of (self-steering) systems that have no particular hierarchical order. Many "mainstream" theoreticians in the tradition of the Western Enlightenment, from Kant to Habermas, used to assume that politics and political institutions are the instruments by which people or human beings can control, steer, or guide society. One may trace this tradition back to Plato's *Republic*. According to Plato, the philosopher kings, due to their superior wisdom and understanding, are supposed to rule society just as the mind is supposed to take control over the body. Already with Plato, there appears a threefold concept of society as a unified body that, by making use of human rationality or reason, can be politically steered. This threefold supposition has remained highly influential in social and political thought up to the present day. Luhmann's theory shares none of the three aspects of such a supposition.

First, Luhmann denies that society is based on unity. Rather, he finds that it is based on distinctions and differences, on the internal differences between social systems and the differences between society and its nonsocial environment. Second, in line with such a focus on multiplicity and difference, Luhmann denies the concept of a general (human) rationality. Instead, he claims that rationality is always the contingent product or construction of a system and that there is no such thing as universal reason. Luhmann pointedly, provocatively, and sarcastically states: "No distinctions-logical concept of rationality would ever lead back to this position of unity and authority. Reason—never again!"[11] Luhmann is here alluding to a famous slogan of the leftist protest movement of the 1970s and 1980s, namely "War—never again!" (*Nie wieder Krieg!*), as well as to Habermas's (who is sometimes perceived as an intellectual spokesperson of this movement) insistence on reason as the universal cure for all social wrongs. Thus, Luhmann ridicules ideological hopes of establishing a new, peaceful, and equal society on the basis of rational politics.

Third, Luhmann attacks the idea that one system in society, namely the political system, can take on a guiding function for all of society. This would imply that the political system or political institutions somehow represent society within society. A political governing body would assume a privileged position within society that would allow society, or, more traditionally, the people, to rule themselves. Luhmann categorically denies such a possibility: "In functionally differentiated societies there is not . . . one unrivalled representation of the society in the society. The political system is thus only able to steer itself by a specific political construction of the difference between system and environment."[12]

Luhmann gives a simple example of the incapability of the political system to steer other systems: "Even relatively simple systems like families pose insurmountable problems to politics if their self-steering is not working. If the family is not able to minimize its differences sufficiently . . . politics is even less able to do so. It can provide the administrative implementation of its own programmes, finance women's refuges, make divorce more or less difficult to obtain, distribute the financial burdens of divorce and by this create deterrents to divorce or ill-considered marriages—in short: do politics. The families themselves cannot be steered in this way."[13]

Politics cannot steer families. While this is perhaps something that even traditional theoreticians might agree with, Luhmann's claim is far more general and does not view the relation between the state and the family as an exceptional case. He is particularly opposed to the idea that society, by means of politics, can steer what politicians in election campaigns (not to speak of socialist and communist states) always promise to be able to steer, namely the (capitalist) economy. Most politicians believe, or at least *claim*, that, if elected, they will be able to make politics benefit the economy. Luhmann, however, maintains: "No policy can renew the economy, parts of the economy or even single firms because for this one needs money and thus the economy."[14] The (capitalist) economy is operationally closed and steers itself. While politics can irritate the economy, that is, cause some economic resonance to political decisions, it cannot steer it.

The self-steering of the (capitalist) economy cannot be planned by politics. That this was true for the socialist and communist experiments has been sufficiently proven by history. That the same holds true for capitalism is not yet a common belief. Here, the dominating semantics still often attribute the capacity of economic steering not to the economic system, but to presidents and finance ministers in the political system. Even if the economic system is taken into account, the traditional humanist semantics still fails to allow for functional-ist perspectives, attributing economical steering to individual hu-man beings such as Alan Greenspan, the big CEOs, or stockbrokers. Luhmann holds that the "economic system cannot be planned, but evolves. While planning takes place it can only influence the historical state to which the system reacts with evolution." He concludes that the "economy produces, on the basis of its self-referential processing in the medium of money and its operational closure, its own dynamics which cannot be controlled politically and to which even the economy can practically only react to after the fact."[15]

Luhmann's claim that there is no central steering agency within society precludes the possibility of immediate political (or scientific) intervention in social processes such as those found in economics. Neither politicians nor economists can set the course for the economy from the outside. Luhmann's argument is, if I understand him cor-rectly, in line with John Gray's criticism of the widespread belief in the efficiency of free market politics. Gray (a professor at the London School of Economics) compares the contemporary free market politics credo to the visions of the French positivists of the nineteenth century (Gray mentions Saint-Simon and Comte) who came up with scientific plans for engineering social and economical progress that, from our perspective today, sound rather grotesque. Gray contends that free market politics, as carried out by institutions such as the International Monetary Fund (IMF), try to impose scientific and political agendas on to economic realties. According to Gray, this has not prevented (and has even perhaps externally contributed to) major economic catas-trophes in Russia and Argentina. Gray summarizes the Argentinean case: "In the aftermath of the IMF's experiment, Argentina is a show-case example of reverse development. The large middle class it once had is ruined. A highly advanced market economy has been replaced by a barter economy. A quarter or more of the population is unem-ployed. Hunger is widespread." And he concludes: "To link exotic fig-ures such as Saint-Simon and Comte with the vapid bureaucrats of the International Monetary Fund may seem fanciful, but the idea of mod-ernization to which the IMF adheres is a Positivist inheritance. The social engineers who labour to install free markets in every last corner of the globe see themselves as scientific rationalists, but they are actually disciples of a forgotten cult."[16]

If human beings cannot steer society, either from within a system or from the outside, through a central agency such as a government or other institutions such as the IMF, then we, as humans, seem to be in a helpless situation—a situation that confronts us with *a fourth insult to human vanity*. Freud had set up a famous list of three insults to human narcissism, namely Copernicus's proof that the earth was not at the center of the universe (the cosmological insult), Darwin's discovery that man was not the crown of creation (the biological insult), and his own findings regarding the insignificant powers of the ego compared with drives and unconscious forces such as the libido (the psychological insult).[17] Luhmann now adds another insult to this list—one that could be called the *sociological insult*. If Luhmann's analysis is correct, then human society cannot steer itself. Just as we cannot control the universe, our bodies, or our minds, we are also unable to shape the social world we inhabit according to our ideals, wishes, or intentions.

How do we cope with this sociological insult? Luhmann's answer is: by creating utopias.[18] These utopias are: "the liberal free market order, socialist welfare justice, social market economy, and the welfare state."[19] In other words: "The political utopia is thus the form by which the uncontrollability of society is copied into the political system."[20] Here, I briefly mention a sarcastic analogy used by Luhmann to illustrate how people deal with the fourth insult. He compares the gestures and promises of the politicians who pretend that they can influence the (capitalist) economy with the rain dances of the Hopi Indians and ascribes the same important function to both, namely "to spread the impression that something is being done rather than merely waiting until things change by themselves."[21] Politics predominantly function symbolically when it comes to the pretension of steering other systems under the conditions of functional differentiation.

One should not underestimate the radicalism of a statement that aims to compare a G8 summit with a Native American ritual. Both are, empirically speaking, quite helpless, and have quite unpredictable effects on the weather and the economy. However, both fulfill key social functions. They not only provide the comfort of feeling that "something is being done," but, and perhaps more importantly, take on great social significance. A rain dance was certainly a major event in Native American religious life. Nowadays, the G8 summit is an event of great international political prestige. Just as someone could, presumably, gain high social status in a Native American community by performing a leading role in a rain dance, to be a speaker at a G8 meeting will not fail to impressively adorn one's political résumé. Both the rain dance and the summit create all kinds of "perturbations" in their respective social environments. They are inevitably the subject of both an Indian family's dinner conversation and CNN prime-time news coverage. A rain dance and a G8 summit are therefore not as interesting for meteorologists or economists as they are for anthropologists and sociologists. It should be added that, from a Luhmannian perspective, neither G8 summits nor rain dances are criticized as useless. Why would an anthropologist or sociologist suggest abandoning these procedures as irrational (as a Habermasian would perhaps do)? They are both important social events in their respective social environments, despite being unable to steer either the weather or the economy.

Luhmann admits that his understanding of the functioning of politics (in analogy to rain dances) radically departs from still-dominant humanist theories. He frankly states that his analysis of the political system leads to "dramatic contradictions" between his theory and "classical conceptions of politics, and particularly of conceptions of democracy."[22] His conclusion that humans cannot steer society and that the political system, which is supposed to manifest the human and rational self-government of human beings, is, strictly speaking, a quasi-religious utopia in the face of the uncontrollability of a (capitalist) economy, is certainly meant as a radical criticism of humanist social self-descriptions. It is *not*, however, meant as a criticism of existing social structures themselves—nor, of course, is it meant as a defense.

Luhmann would not say that G8 summits or rain dances are entirely irrational and should therefore be abolished. He thinks of them in purely functionalist terms and criticizes an understanding of their functioning in humanist terms. This complacency with the present status quo has earned Luhmann many criticisms for being a conservative.[23] I would, however, read Luhmann in a different way. Connecting back to the beginning of this section and the later Luhmann's own self-designations, I claim that Luhmann is—although less "critical"—more radical than many current post-Marxists such as, for instance, Michael Hardt and Antonio Negri, who represent what could be called the radical left in the context of contemporary Western social theory. What makes thinkers of the radical left less radical is that they often share humanist patterns with the "rightist" or liberal thinkers whom they argue against. Hardt and Negri, for instance, have a far more humanist vision of democracy and are rooted in the Enlightenment tradition to a greater extent than Luhmann. Even if they no longer use some of the old-fashioned concepts like the "people" or the "masses," but a postmodernist variation of it, namely (in their case), the "multitude," they continue to dream of theoretically contributing to an improved society that is more democratic, more equal, and more just than the world at present; ultimately, they are hoping for a new communism to be realized. Such an approach may well be labeled radical in the context of liberal political theory. But, after all, communism is not exactly an ideology that radically departs from common political ideas and ideals of the nineteenth and twentieth centuries; it simply is one of the more "fundamentalist" forms within the Western Enlightenment political spectrum. While thinkers like Hardt and Negri try to modify nineteenth- and twentieth-century thought to make it more applicable in the twenty-first century, the basic premises of political thought remain the same, namely that political thought explores the social structures of oppression that prevent people from living a better, that is, more free, powerful, and just life. In this sense, authors like Hardt and Negri represent a radical wing *within* the mainstream tradition of modern Western political theory.

Luhmann's provocative "sociological insult" of human vanity looks to both the established political system and the protest movements, activisms, and theories that consider themselves to be in opposition to this establishment or "the system." In fact, from a Luhmannian perspective, both the established political parties and the so-called NGOs, both the Republicans and Greenpeace, both the G8 summit and the demonstrations against it in the streets constitute the political system and share the belief that humans can and should politically steer society. They only disagree on the means and ends of political steering; they only differ with respect to their position of power. Neither the government nor the opposition (no matter if in Parliament or on the streets) accepts the "limits of steering."[24] Luhmann's analysis offers the possibilities for a much more fundamental paradigm shift than ordinary political activism and protest, even if it may not offer seemingly radical practical solutions. A mere attempt at offering a practical solution to the traditional problems identified by modern political and social theory cannot yet be called radical. If the questions remain exactly the same, how can the answers expected to be radically different?

Luhmann's analysis of society radically departs from a lot of the basic premises of mainstream modern political theory. This creative potential of his theory is, among other things, what I explore in this book. Just as the cosmological, the biological, and the psychological insults did in the past, Luhmann's sociological insult may well be seen as enabling theory to move forward and leave certain intellectual tracks behind. It cannot be known where this new way of looking at the world will lead, but it might be worth exploring, if only for the sake of trying something less boring.[25] Social systems theory does not deal with fabricating new hopes, new promises, or new utopias, but it is also not afraid of letting go of hopes that cannot be fulfilled, promises that have never been kept, and fairytale visions of a golden future. It dares to introduce a nonhumanist paradigm shift in social theory—one that may "perturb" society in a profound and (obviously) entirely contingent way.

Mere criticisms do not challenge the dominating self-descriptions of society as much as a paradigm shift does. Critical theory typically decries that certain ideals have not yet been sufficiently realized and need another try. In a way, critical theory thus serves the conservative project of finishing the yet unfinished project of enlightenment. Social systems theory, to the contrary, is "metacritical" in its critical departure from critical theory.[26] Luhmann, in a fashion similar to Copernicus, Darwin, and Freud, shatters some of the "commonsense" self-descriptions so that previously unimagined possibilities of looking at the world can emerge.

FOUR

FROM NECESSITY TO CONTINGENCY
A CARNIVALIZATION OF PHILOSOPHY

Niklas Luhmann's relation to the discipline and history of philosophy was highly ambiguous. He was "officially" a sociologist (a professor in a department of sociology) and always regarded himself as one. However, he was awarded one of the most prestigious philosophy prizes in Germany, the Hegel Award, in 1989, and in his works he referred to Plato and Kant at least as often as to the works of the sociological founding fathers. Jürgen Habermas rightly stated: "It is not so much the disciplinary tradition of social theory from Comte to Parsons that Luhmann tries to connect up with, as the history of problems associated with the philosophy of consciousness from Kant to Husserl."[1]

In *Die Gesellschaft der Gesellschaft* Luhmann says: "If one intends to pass a judgment on the possibilities for self-description in and by modern society, one must most of all take into account that this self-description is no longer transmitted orally in the form of teachings of wisdom and also no longer articulates lofty ultimate thoughts in the form of philosophy. It rather follows the particular rules of the mass media. Every morning and every evening the web of news is inescapably lowered down on earth and determines what has been and what one has to be aware of."[2]

This is a sarcastic, or rather a "carnivalesque" statement, since, in the terms of Mikhail Bakhtin, it unites the sacred with the profane, the high with the low, and the wise with the foolish.[3] Traditionally, the sages, the priests, and the men of wisdom were responsible for informing society about itself, for explaining the world. Later on, philosophers assumed this function. Nowadays, however, the mass media have taken over. Most people consult neither the wise nor the philosophy professors to be told what matters. Most people simply switch on the TV (or, since times have quickly changed, the computer). Philosophy used to be the love of wisdom. With Hegel, it was supposed to become more than that, namely "actual knowing" or science (*Wissenschaft*).[4] Hegel understood this transformation as an "elevation" (*Erhebung*). After the rise, however, we have to conclude with Luhmann, came the fall. Philosophy was soon replaced by the mass media as the main purveyor of "actual knowledge."

The mass media are in fact not the only source of society's self-description, of course, although they are probably the most important. The statement quoted above is, for rhetorical reasons, exaggerated. After all, Luhmann's whole theory is supposed to be another self-description in and of society as well. In this way, not only the mass media can claim to be the usurper of "Hegel's throne," but also Luhmann himself.[5]

Hegel is not only among the most referenced philosophers in Luhmann's works, he also shares a key term with Luhmann: "system." Hegel followed Kant's transcendental methodology, distinguishing between a (scientific) system and a mere aggregate of information that for him did not count as true science. A mere aggregate of information is simply a collection or assembly of facts. As such, it cannot claim to be scientific. Knowledge becomes scientific once it is systematized, once it is integrated into a coherent whole. The most decisive difference between a mere aggregate of information and a scientific system is that the former is coincidental whereas the latter is necessary. A collection of information, such as a compilation of statistical data about body temperature, is only a random collection of numbers as long as it is not understood within an overarching conceptual scheme. Once medical concepts and principles are applied, the data can be related to each other and constitute a scientific description of, for instance, a fever. Seen within a larger conceptual context, the temperature data become "necessary" by becoming part of a specific medical history. The body temperature becomes a necessary aspect of the health of a patient. For Hegel, the concepts of philosophy, science, system, and necessity are mutually explanatory. True philosophy has to be scientific; science is by definition systematic; and that which is systematic is understood as necessary: "the True is actual only as system."[6]

The science that Hegel was interested in, which for him was the only true science, was the "science of the experience of consciousness," or, in other words, the phenomenology of spirit. For Hegel, science, in its ultimate meaning was the process of the self-understanding of consciousness. Through science, consciousness understands its own necessity (in Hegel's sense of this term). It understands itself, its history, its structure, and its manifestations in a systematic fashion and comes to grasp its own necessity. Science is not primarily concerned with information about objects external to itself, but is instead the cognition of cognition. Science is self-reflective. True science, and here Hegel once again continues the Kantian tradition, is reason's enlightenment of itself. In Luhmannian terms, one can say that philosophy, for Hegel, consisted in the systematic, and therefore scientific, self-description of spirit through which spirit realizes (in the twofold meaning of this term) its own necessity and reality. Only spirit has the capacity to be self-reflective in this manner. As long as consciousness or thought is concerned with the (seemingly) nonspiritual it remains in an alienated state (and this necessitates the subjective turn of philosophical science). It can only fully realize itself in and through itself. The highest type of cognition is the self-cognition of cognition. This is what scientific and systematic philosophy consists in. It is the ultimate self-description. For Hegel, any attempt at self-description had to culminate in (t)his philosophical system.

If my understanding is correct, and philosophy, for Hegel, was the ultimate (or absolute) self-description—not of himself, of course, but in general—then one may well conceive of Luhmann's project, in light of the above quotation, as a "carnivalization" (in Bakhtin's terms) or *Aufhebung* (in Hegelian terms) of Hegel. I will show how Luhmann ironically twisted the Hegelian approach and thereby "deconstructed" traditional philosophy. In order to do this, I briefly summarize my reading of Hegel.

For Hegel, philosophy was the ultimate self-description that is

Spiritual. As the grammatically ambiguous title *Phenomenology of Spirit* demonstrates, philosophy is both performed *by* the spirit and *about* it. Philosophy is spirit relating to itself. Spirit manifests itself as conscious cognition. It is, substantially speaking, ideal, and not material. Spirit realizes itself in consciousness.

Scientific. Philosophy is the most fundamental and highest form of science or knowledge. Only philosophy is concerned with "the True" (with a capital T).[7] All other sciences, with mathematics and history as paradigmatic examples, are in a state of alienation in which their objects do not coincide with their mode of cognition. All of the truths they arrive at remain external and partial. Only philosophical science is able to grasp truth wholly; only it can comprehend nothing less than "the entire realm of the truth of Spirit."[8]

Systematic. Philosophy is the only truly systematic science and, therefore, strictly speaking, the only real science. Only the philosophical system includes itself completely in itself. Its principles do not remain axiomatic, but become fully integrated into the systemic whole. A complete system is not a linear, hierarchical chain of argumentation, but a coherent and circular whole in which all aspects are equally foundational.

Necessary. Only philosophy is a complete scientific system, and therefore only philosophy establishes complete necessity. Philosophy is not concerned with a simple registering of isolated facts that could be otherwise, but with a systemic understanding of contextual necessity.

Like Hegel, Luhmann was concerned with self-description, and, like Hegel, he was concerned with systems. However, an obvious difference should be stated right away in order to avoid any misunderstanding: while Hegel believed that his philosophy took on the shape of a system, Luhmann's systems theory is a theory *about* systems and not a system itself (although it obviously emerges within a contemporary social system, namely the science system). The entities that Luhmann called systems, that is, social systems, biological systems, psychic systems, and so on, are *not* systems in the Hegelian sense of the term.

For Hegel, there was, strictly speaking, only one real system, namely his own philosophy. For Luhmann, systems are empirically given, and they comprise such manifold things as cells, the economy, and people's minds. Hegel understood the concept of system in the Kantian sense as the ideal (and only true) form of science (as opposed to a mere aggregate of information), whereas for Luhmann (autopoietic) systems were self-generating and self-reproducing operational processes. The Hegelian and Luhmannian usages of the term "system" have little in common.

Similarities emerge, however, if one compares Hegel's system with Luhmann's concept of theory. While Hegel aimed at constructing a stringent and coherent philosophical system, Luhmann aimed at establishing a general and encompassing social theory. Luhmann often stated that he conceived of himself as a theorist, and *Social Systems* has (in the German edition) *Outline of a General Theory* as its subtitle. He was never specific in defining what exactly a theory is, but perhaps that was supposed to be self-evident. In one of the passages in which he talks about his theory as a theory, he uses a telling metaphor. At the end of *Einführung in die Systemtheorie* (Introduction to Systems Theory) he speaks of "theory architecture" and "problems of design."[9] Theory is understood as a conceptual edifice, or, as he explains on the same page, as concepts within a coherent context of usage. Kant used exactly the same metaphor in his transcendental methodology and spoke about the "architecture of pure reason" and the "art of systems."[10] It is probably safe to say that Luhmann's theory is a successor of Kant's and Hegel's system. Luhmann did not intend to be a "normal science" sociologist, helping to increase the sociological "aggregate of information" by conducting surveys and collecting data. Instead, he wanted to react to the theory crisis in sociology and establish a new general theory of society.[11]

If one compares Luhmann's concept of theory with Hegel's concept of the system, then one can point out at least four similarities:

1. Both system and theory are meant to be *begrifflich durchkonstruiert*,[12] which means they have to be both "conceptual" and "thoroughly constructed." Theory and system are based on notions, not on facts, and

they have to constitute a coherent and comprehensive network, a consistent whole.

2. Both system and theory are meant to be universally applicable. While not being concerned with mere "naked truths" (*nackte Wahrheiten*, an expression used by Hegel for the facts that traditional historiography deals with, such as, for instance, the date of Caesar's birth),[13] system and theory are capable of identifying the meaning of basically any event within their respective conceptual framework. Hegel was not interested in Caesar's birthday, but he could identify the significance of Caesar's existence in terms of his philosophical apparatus. Similarly, Luhmann's theory was supposed to be so encompassing that it was able to interpret something so mundane as the dynamics of a soccer game in the terms of social systems theory.[14]

3. Both system and theory are concerned with an adequate understanding of their subjects, or at least a more adequate understanding than that of previous philosophers or sociologists. For Hegel, the philosophical system was the only adequate form of science. He did not accuse his philosophical predecessors of being wrong or false, but he viewed them as lacking in conceptual refinement. Hegel was not concerned with discovering new facts or with simply refuting others. He conceived of his task in the fashion of Jesus Christ: his system was not meant to falsify the earlier prophets, but to substantially raise the level of expression and thus to present the same truth in a more adequate fashion.[15] Luhmann was certainly less religious than Hegel, and his striving for adequacy was less ambitious. Still, Luhmann was hoping that his theory might surpass all of its competitors in adequacy. He did not want to suggest yet another version of a prescriptive social theory (in addition to, for instance, Marx and Habermas) and accused those who accused him of not offering any help or advice to society of betraying theoretical adequacy with their political agendas. Rather than telling society what to do and where to go, he intended to improve the adequacy of social theory by raising it above and beyond ideology.[16]

4. The most intricate similarity between Hegel's system and Luhmann's theory relates to their respective claims of self-inclusion. By way of a conceptual feedback loop both are supposed to finally explain themselves through themselves. Hegel's goal in the *Phenomenology* is

"Absolute Knowing, or Spirit that knows itself as Spirit".[17] In the end the system realizes that it is its own content, that it can only be truly complete by completely including itself. Luhmann seems to deny this self-inclusion to Hegel's system when he writes: "The novel, the romance, but also Hegel's novel of the love between world-history and philosophy localizes the observer who can also see what he himself previously could not see at the end of the story. This makes it necessary to exclude the narrator who has known everything already from the beginning, and thus also Hegel himself, from the story."[18] I do not think that this criticism is fair. As I see it, the main characteristic of the system in Hegel's *Phenomenology* (the "novel of the love between world-history and philosophy") is precisely such an *Insichgehen* (withdrawal into itself)[19] in which the narration, and thus the narrator, finally turns out to be its own *subject*. In any case, Luhmann explicitly claims such a self-inclusion for his theory: "In this way, the epistemologist becomes him/herself a rat in the labyrinth and has to reflect on the position from which he/she observes the other rats. Then, the reflection no longer merely leads to the common conditions, but beyond these to the unity of the system of cognition, and all 'externalization' has to be explained as system-differentiation. Only with the sociology of cognition does a radical, self-inclusive constructivism become possible."[20] Luhmann's radical constructivism refers back to itself. Indeed, it radically constructs itself. The theory is about cognitive construction (including and focusing on social construction), but also realizes that it is within society and thus within the construction it is about. The problem with self-inclusion is therefore the most decisive aspect that theory and system have in common. However, the problem of self-inclusion leads to radically different consequences for Hegel and Luhmann and, by extension, for system and theory. It is not only what makes them similar, but also what distinguishes them. It is here too that I think we find clear evidence for Luhmann's radicalism.

For Hegel, philosophy was ultimately the science (*Wissenschaft*) of the spirit (*Geist*)—both in a subjective and an objective sense, that is, both by and about spirit. Spirit manifests itself as knowledge (*Wissen*) and as cognition (*Erkenntnis*), and, as the science of the "experience of consciousness." Philosophy is therefore cognitive science, and, in a very strict sense, *Geisteswissenschaft* (literally: science of the spirit). The term *Geisteswissenschaft,* however, also means in a broader and more contemporary sense the humanities (as opposed to, for instance, *Naturwissenschaften,* or natural sciences). Derived from the Hegelian concept of philosophy as the foundational "science of the spirit," the other *Geisteswissenschaften* were conceived of as dealing with more specific manifestations of spirit (such as history, arts, languages, etc.) This conceptual model implies, in the Hegelian sense, that spirit is the underlying intelligent or cognitive principle of (human) reality. Spirit is cognitive, and all (human) activity is substantially cognitive or spiritual. Luhmann stood in strong opposition to subsuming everything human under a general notion such as spirit. He flatly opposed this Hegelian heritage: "The ambition of a common foundation, a foundational symbol, an ultimate thought, has to be abandoned—or left to the philosophers. Sociology does not get—in any case not in this way—to what Hegel had called 'spirit.' It is not a *Geisteswissenschaft.*"[21]

While Luhmann continued to understand society in terms of *cognition,* he no longer agreed with Hegel and other humanists that cognition is to be understood as something founded on spirit.[22] Luhmann says, quite sarcastically, that if one intends to continue to believe in one universal "ultimate thought" that underlies all (human) activity one may still be a philosopher in the traditional sense, but not, as Hegel had assumed, a (social) scientist. By separating cognition from spirit, Luhmann thus implicitly also separated philosophy from (social) science. In Luhmann's theory, cognition is systemic and can be spiritual (or, as Luhmann would say, mental), but it can also be social and biological—or, perhaps, "machinic," chemical, and so on. For Luhmann, social systems can cognize as much as minds or cells can, but there is no "common foundation" for these types of cognition. A science of cognition is therefore no longer a "science of the spirit." Sociology, for Luhmann, is concerned with the cognition of social systems, but it is not concerned with spirit or even with humans. It is not philosophy nor does it belong to *Geisteswissenschaften* in the Hegelian sense.

For Hegel, there were, in the strict sense, no sciences in the plural. Science was a unified endeavor with philosophy at its helm. This was not the case for Luhmann. Science, for Luhmann, has emerged as a social system along with the development of functional differentiation. Modern science is thus a function system next to others such as law, politics, economy, and so on. Luhmann was interested in how this system functions. He wrote a lengthy monograph on the subject—*The Science of Society*.[23] While this is not the place to outline Luhmann's analysis of science as a social system, it may suffice to say that, like other systems, science has its own code (true/false), programs (theories, models), function (production of knowledge), and so on. Like other systems, it provides opportunities for careers (professors, scientists) and is structurally coupled with various systems such as (manifested in the systemically hybrid organization of the contemporary university) the education system, the economy, and, in the United States, even sports.

Embedding science in society removes the exalted prestige that it enjoyed with Hegel as well as the identification of science with philosophy. Science has, in modern society, no privilege whatsoever over any other system. One becomes more famous in sports, for instance. Despite producing knowledge, science does not produce general knowledge. This function is assumed by the mass media. That which is "known to be known"[24] is what we know through watching TV and browsing the Internet, not what is published in academic journals. There is no particular importance ascribed to philosophy in the sciences. No physicist will be employed because of her excellent knowledge of Plato. Philosophy still enjoys some traditional prestige, but it certainly does not have a definite or guiding influence on the other sciences. Luhmann points out that nowadays it is entirely out of the question that philosophy can claim to be the leading scientific discipline.[25]

Like Hegel, Luhmann conceived of himself as a scientist. While for Hegel this meant that he was replacing the priests in expressing the world-spirit, for Luhmann it meant that he was publishing in an autopoietic and operationally closed system of communication that produces texts and theories that are selected for publication on the basis of such criteria as true or false rather than, for instance, on the basis of "selectors" such as being scandalous or not (as in the mass media).[26] For Hegel, (philosophical) science was the highest form of cognitive or spiritual activity. For Luhmann, it was a type of communication that had evolved among many others. Interestingly enough, both scientists were very much aware of the paradoxical nature of their scientific endeavors—which is most obviously expressed in the grammatically ambiguous titles of their major works (*The Phenomenology of Spirit* and the many works by Luhmann that are titled analogously: *The Science of Society, The Politics of Society, The Society of Society,* etc.).[27] The type of science they pursued included itself in itself. For Hegel, the science of the spirit was a science both by and about spirit. For Luhmann, the study of society could only be performed within society by a sociologist. The theory of social systems is itself a product of one of the systems, namely science, which it analyzes. Rephrasing the quotation from above, it can be said that the scientist becomes himself a rat in the labyrinth that science has constructed.

It is crucial to note how this scientific feedback loop is connected with two diametrically opposed assessments of the status of the Hegelian system on the one hand and Luhmannian theory on the other. To analyze this difference I contrast Hegel's ending of the preface to the *Phenomenology* with that found in Luhmann's *Science of Society.* Hegel ends his preface with a pseudo-modest reflection on how he, the individual philosopher, is only a spokesperson for the "universality of Spirit" that chose to express itself through him. I am saying "pseudo-modest" because while Hegel downplays his own role in the self-realization of spirit, he nevertheless is very clear about the fact that his is the time at which the "universality of Spirit" has finally "gathered such strength" as it never did before. Hegel claims nothing less than embodying the culmination of spirit's self-realization. While Hegel admits that Spirit could have expressed itself through another individual philosopher, he nevertheless implies that it would not have failed to express itself in the form of the philosophical system that was published under his name.[28]

Luhmann's preface to *The Science of Society*, on the other hand, ends on a distinctively different note, namely, if my interpretation of its cryptic last sentence is appropriate, with self-irony. Luhmann concludes his acknowledgements of colleagues and students by stating: "It remains only to say, as usual, that any remaining errors are chargeable to me—with the exception of errors in this sentence, obviously!"

When one reads the first half of this sentence, one expects Luhmann to be doing what most authors of academic publications do, that is, making a personal gesture of moral responsibility toward others, after just having expressed equally personal feelings of gratitude and affection toward them, in a specific section of a book (usually the preface or the acknowledgments) which, in its main parts, is scientific and thus impersonal, unemotional, and amoral. This expectation is then radically disappointed (a common technique for jokes) in the second half of the sentence. In the light of the second half of the sentence, the seemingly personal, emotional, and ethical statements of academic authors in the acknowledgments are exposed as simply or "obviously" one more stereotype within academic or scientific writing and thus as having nothing to do with *individual* feelings or moral convictions. They are thus just as much a linguistic convention enforced on academic authors by the science system as the academic jargon used in the main body of the book. In other words, acknowledgments are not simply authentic personal, emotional, and moral confessions that demonstrate some personal traits of the author, but one more stereotypical form of expression constructed within the discourse of academic writing. In fact, such seemingly personal statements—being so stereotypical—demonstrate the very opposite of what they state, namely that scientific communication operates "systemically" in accordance with the codes, programs, and communicative conventions it has developed and therefore does not leave room for personal emotions or moral authenticity. In this way, the final sentence of the preface of *The Science of Society* demonstrates, in the form of a *parody*, that science is *not* the authentic realization of truth, but a social system with its own standardized forms of communication, just like all other social systems. Its "truth" is merely a communicative construct among many others.

This brings me to what is, to my mind, the most important difference between Hegel and Luhmann: the status they ascribed to science. Hegel conceived of (philosophical) science as a system of *necessity* and Luhmann understood (sociological) science as a theory of *contingency*.

The German word used by Hegel for necessity is *Notwendigkeit.* Literally, the German noun *Not,* etymologically related to the English noun *need,* indicates a state of crisis or emergency. A *Hungersnot,* for instance, is a famine—a critical situation in which people are hungry, that is, there is a *need* for food that cannot be met, and thus there is *hunger.* The German noun *Wende,* on the other hand, which is the linguistic root of the *wendigkeit* part of *Notwendigkeit,* means "turn" or "shift." In a *Hungersnot,* when people are hungry and thus need food, they feel the *necessity* to eat so that the situation of *need* will be *turned* into or *shifted* toward a situation without need. In this way, *notwendig* means "necessary" not merely in a logical or modal sense, but rather in an existential sense, where something is needed in order to resolve a crisis. When one is hungry, it is *necessary* to eat. A quite appropriate English translation for the term "necessary" in Hegel's usage would therefore be "critical."

In the *Phenomenology of Spirit,* a book that Luhmann has called "the great novel of philosophy,"[29] Hegel recalls (*erinnert*) the *Bildung* (roughly, "growth" or "maturation") of spirit. In this sense, it is a sort of *autobiographic novel* of spirit.[30] Hegel's main task in this book is to reconstruct the "necessity" of all experiences throughout the life of spirit. This is *not* to say that he is pursuing the project of explaining why everything was predestined from the beginning and therefore modally necessary rather than merely accidental or possible. Instead, in connection with the existential meaning of "necessary," he intends to explore the "critical meaning" of whatever happened to, with, and by spirit.

In our personal lives, for instance, we may pursue the project of trying to understand our experiences in such a way—not as being predestined, but as necessary elements that have made us into what we are now. We can look at our life as a series of "needful" situations in which we acted in accordance with those needs. We can understand, for instance, why and that we needed to marry our partner, why and that we needed to become a professor, why and that we needed to have or to not have children, and so on. We only understand ourselves and our life fully once we completely understand the necessity of all we have done. If we successfully recall our growth and maturation, the experiences of our life, then we will be able to conceive of every moment as a necessary step to what we have finally become. The past events of one's life will all connect to each other and be recognized as meaningful with respect to what one is now. It is no longer merely coincidental and thus ultimately senseless that, for instance, one married, had a child or two, or met this or that friend. All these experiences become important and decisive parts of what one is.

Hegel, in the *Phenomenology of Spirit,* attempted to describe the necessities of the life of spirit or the experience of consciousness. This experience was to be understood as being constituted by *critical turning points,* and in this sense it was to lose its contingency. A complete self-understanding means a complete transformation of the status of our experience from being seemingly contingent and accidental events into a meaningful and necessary whole. Hegel aspired to perform such a *transformation of contingency into necessity* not for his personal life, but for the whole life or experience of spirit, that is, the world. That was the task of philosophy, of systematic science.

Just as "necessity" is a crucial concept for Hegel, "contingency" is central for Luhmann. The word contingency, like the word "necessity," has a certain ambiguity to it and for Luhmann a particular meaning. "Contingent" means "contingent upon" or "depending on." I can say: I will attend this conference in Montreal, but it will be contingent upon my flight to Montreal not being unexpectedly canceled. In this sense, the term means, as does its Latin origin, to "hang together with" or "to be connected with." Two things depend on one another and are tied to one another: my attendance at the conference and the plane's reaching Montreal. Either both will come true or neither of them. It is not coincidental or purely by chance that I will appear at the conference, but essentially related to that flight not being canceled. In this sense, it is not against all odds or unlikely that I will appear at the conference, but rather probable. Once the plane for Montreal had departed it became more or less certain that, in connection with this fact, I would attend the conference (contingent upon the plane not crashing, of course).

"Contingent," however, also means "not necessary" or "by chance," in the sense that "it could have come about otherwise." If I say that it was a matter of pure contingency that my father married my mother and that I was subsequently born, this could be meant, for instance, in this way: if my father's car had not unexpectedly broken down in that town on that day, had he not ended up in that particular bar that night, and met my mother, chances are that they would never have met at all and that I would not have been born. It is purely a matter of chance that I exist—and, in fact, considering the probabilities of all the unintended and unplanned things that had to happen for my father to meet my mother that night, my existence was basically against all odds or "extremely unlikely" to use a phrase often employed by Luhmann.

"Contingent" for Luhmann means both "being connected with" and "extremely unlikely." Given the fact that I do exist, that I became an academic who specializes in Luhmann, that I was invited to this conference on Luhmann in Montreal, that my application for a travel grant was successful, and that the flight to Montreal was not canceled, my attendance was no surprise. Given all other possibilities, however, and the very fact of the utter improbability of my existence in the first place, the fact that I appeared at this conference in Montreal was indeed against all odds. Contingency, for Luhmann, does not simply mean "anything goes" or "pure coincidence." It means that whatever happens is connected with many other things. At the same time, however, it is also extremely unlikely any given things should happen because of all the contingencies involved.

Luhmann, as a theoretician of contingency, did not believe in the possibility of a master-narrative such as the one Hegel aspired to in the *Phenomenology*. Hegel wanted to tell the narrative of spirit. By *transforming contingency into necessity*, we end up with a coherent story, with a unified whole. While Hegel believed that the complete self-inclusion, or feedback loop, of science or philosophy would lead to the self-unification of spirit and an insight into its own necessity, for Luhmann (and many postmodernist thinkers) this "project of modernity" has to be abolished. Luhmann believed that insight into the scientific feedback loop demonstrates contingency and not ultimate necessity. There is no necessity for science to have become what it is. There was no necessity for our society to develop as it had. That all the social phenomena experienced today exist is even more *unlikely* than my personal existence, which was against all odds. Other possibilities were and always are there. There were societies that had no science, no economy, and not even families—and there will likely be future societies in which all these social formations will no longer be what they are today. Given their connection with everything that has happened in the past few hundred years, we can explain why all the social phenomena are as they are and why things evolved the way they did.

For Luhmann, science is the opposite of what it was for Hegel; it is the *transformation of necessity into contingency*. It is the discovery of the unlikely within the familiar. Luhmann therefore approaches social theory in a very different way from Western mainstream philosophers, from Hobbes to Habermas, who often presumed they might find some meaningful (normative or natural or rational) foundation for social reality. The modern state, for instance, could be seen as a necessary reaction to the crisis of what Hobbes famously called the "natural" war of all against all. Social institutions, like politics, the economy, the family, and so on, could therefore become "necessary" in a Hegelian sense for mainstream modern theoreticians. From the perspective of these thinkers, social philosophy can show us why and how, for instance, our basic laws and our political constitutions are grounded on certain necessities. Social science has the function of explaining these necessities and further developing social institutions in accordance with them.

Luhmann questioned this necessity, viewing society instead as a complex dynamic system in which meaning is always contingent and subject to construction. The meaning of social institutions and values is derived from their connection with other social institutions and values that have happened to evolve. There is no ultimate necessity to them given that they are all so extremely unlikely. For instance, there is no existential or natural or rational necessity for our legal and political institutions. In the context of our current society, they are of course explicable and understandable, but, at the same time, they are entirely unnecessary in a Hegelian sense. We can see that things could potentially be very different.

The theoretical consequence of Luhmann's discovery of utter contingency was not to declare a complete arbitrariness of "anything goes," but to replace a philosophy of necessity with a theory of contingency. For him, the switch from a program of transforming contingency into necessity to a program of transforming necessity into contingency did not mean the end of social theory, but rather a new beginning.

Luhmann described his position as such: "We would gladly concede that there is no such thing as a binding representation of a society within that society. But that concession would be not the end but rather the beginning of a reflection on the form of such a system's own self-observations and self-descriptions. These must be submitted within the system in a process that must in turn be observed and described."[31]

The lack of a "binding representation of a society within that society" means that there is no metanarrative, no Hegelian recollection, that would unite all social phenomena within one phenomeno-*logy*. This may well be the end of the possibility for any philosophical system in the Hegelian sense. However, for Luhmann, it meant the beginning of a theory of the impossibility of metanarratives, a theory of self-descriptions in a feedback loop, a theory of self-descriptions that are contingent upon themselves. Rather than understanding how a society functions on the basis of necessity, Luhmann wants to understand how it can, and indeed does, function on the basis of contingency.

Against the background of this comparison between Hegel and Luhmann, this quotation from Luhmann should gain a more particular significance: "If one intends to pass a judgment on the possibilities for self-description in and by modern society, one must most of all take into account that this self-description is no longer transmitted orally in the form of teachings of wisdom and also no longer articulates lofty ultimate thoughts in the form of philosophy."[32]

The replacement of a "lofty" system of necessity with a theory of contingency is a replacement of an outdated form of science with a new form of science. It marks the end of the assumption that a scientific self-description is actually an "elevation" (*Erhebung*) at all. Luhmann's self-description is neither "wise" nor "philosophical" in the traditional sense. It is one of many possible self-descriptions emerging within the feedback loop of contingent forms of communication. It lacks any transcendent or enlightening qualities. It is a paradoxical insight into the impossibility of any elevation or definite enlightenment.

Philosophy, therefore, to put it in Hegelian terms, has passed the point of its highest purpose. It can no longer be accepted as what it once believed it was: the most foundational scientific knowledge. Therefore, philosophy is now just one of the many disciplines taught at academic institutions and paid for by students, the government, or both. Luhmann summarizes the actual state of this discipline quite accurately: "Some philosophers are now only interested in the textual history of the discipline, others in fashionable topics such as postmodernism or ethics; still others present the predicament of any general view in a literary or feuilleton-like way; and, what is perhaps worst: the striving for precision that borders on pedantry."[33]

The time of the philosophical system is past. One can still work in the field as a curator of the dusty classics; one can take part in discourses or debates that have proven to be intellectually marketable (postmodernism, ethics); one can do away with the scientific pretension altogether and write texts that are pleasant to read; or one can do the opposite and assume a seriously scientific attitude and write technical papers that do not say much. This last possibility, also known as analytic philosophy, seems to currently dominate the field, at least in North America, but Luhmann did not find it very attractive. Given this state of affairs, Luhmann concludes: "What once was philosophy thus degenerates to a mere expertise in dealing with philosophical texts, and philosophers become experts in philosophy."[34]

There is no social role left for the wise men and the philosophers of old. Neither wise sayings nor the establishing of the ultimate scientific system will help one in pursuing an academic career, not even in philosophy. Instead, one has to engage in a variation of the four types of academic philosophy described above and become a professional expert. Hegel himself would probably have found it difficult to get through the contemporary peer review process: I would be curious to find out which publisher would accept the manuscript of the *Phenomenology of Spirit* today. Luhmann seems to be a bit nostalgic about this and to feel more akin to his philosophical (and perhaps even wise) predecessors than to the academic experts of his day.

If neither philosophy nor science can claim to be the "binding representation of a society within that society," there is no such thing as a foundational self-description of society. Luhmann's theory, however, claims to be a self-description, but a self-description of a social state in which no foundational self-descriptions are possible. He is therefore quick to admit that other social self-descriptions outside of science may well be more influential than his own. This brings us back to Luhmann's assertion that the self-description in and by modern society "follows the particular rules of the mass media. Every morning and every evening the web of news is inescapably lowered down on earth and determines what has been and what one has to be aware of."[35]

Sociology is not more real, venerable, or "True" (with a capital T) than the news, the weather report, or even a commercial. It is more "true" in the sense that truth/falsity is the basic code of the system of science. Scientific communication normally discusses the truth-value of scientific propositions, like this book, which attempts to represent Hegel and Luhmann truly and tries to point out certain falsities as well. If I should be lucky enough to have this book eventually generate further scientific communication, it will be typically about the truth/falsity of my propositions, and so on in a spiral of communicative autopoiesis. The mass media, on the other hand, have other priorities. Presenting spectacular information, for instance, is more important than assessing truth/falsity.[36] On the night before I wrote this, I heard an interview with a U.S. university professor of anatomy who believed in and hoped to prove the existence of Big Foot. This scientist freely admitted that he was having a hard time gaining respect in the academic community. But he obviously found it much easier to attract the attention of the mass media than did most of his colleagues. The mass media are not so much interested in Big Foot as a subject that promises to bring about new "truths"; they are more interested in presenting interesting information. The mass media system and the science system construct different self-descriptions of society that are not compatible with each other since they communicate differently and on the basis of incommensurable codes, programs, and so on. There is no single system that can impose its codes and constructions on others. Luhmann's theory tries to address this paradox. Science has to make true propositions about the impossibility of truth under current social conditions.

This paradoxical situation leads to a carnivalization of philosophy and science. That which was once esteemed (or, more precisely, esteemed itself) as the lofty mountain top of human cognition, appears as only one contingent reality construction among many. The difference between the high and the low has been removed. The carnival used to make fun of the aristocrats and clerics and expose their pretensions. Theory makes fun of science and philosophy and exposes their pretensions. In a somewhat Socratic manner, social theory explains its own limits and thereby the limits of any attempt at knowledge. If my interpretation is correct, Luhmann labeled his own theory a "super-theory" in a self-ironic fashion.[37] This interpretation is supported by the peculiar style of Luhmann's texts in which one finds dry, technical, and conceptual language frequently interspersed with bits of sarcasm, satire, and parody.[38]

I would argue that the traditional scientific-philosophical ambitions of the enlightenment have been undermined by carnivalistic theory and that this leads to a certain "lightness of being," or, alternatively, *la gaya scienza*. One can witness the "dialectics of enlightenment" brought about by the scientific age. With indubitable Cartesian scientific "certainty," and with utmost seriousness, the great projects of social science were put into practice: the French rule of reason, the Russian elimination of class distinctions, the racism of the Nazis, the disciplinary mechanisms described by Foucault—these were all supported and defended by what may be called "extremist" science, philosophy, or both. Today, we see the applications of their supposedly more rational successors: free markets expanding worldwide along with neo-Kantian universal recipes for peace, social understanding, and liberty. If faced with a choice between these types of serious science and carnivalistic theory, I'd find it rather easy to decide in favor of the latter.

FIVE

THE LAST FOOTNOTE TO PLATO
A SOLUTION TO THE MIND-BODY PROBLEM

One of the most useful of Luhmann's radicalisms is what I would dare to call nothing less than a convincing solution to the mind-body problem that has haunted the history of ideas in the West for two and a half millennia.[1] Given the contingent character of the theory, it should be noted right away that this is not to say it is the solution to *the* mind-body problem. Luhmann's solution to this problem necessarily arises from the contingency of the problem: it is part of the semantic heritage or history that Luhmann's theory relates to. The problem is, to begin with, not so much a substantial problem as a conceptual one. As always, "solution" can only mean: an observational construct. Such a solution "solves" a problem in a Wittgensteinian sense, namely by increasing the clarity of the terminology and thereby reducing the "abuse" of language.

The history of the mind-body dualism dates back to Plato, to the *Phaedo*, the *Republic*, and other of his major works. This dualism has at least three dimensions. First, an *ontological* distinction between different ways of being: physical and intellectual being. Whatever is, is either physical or intellectual, or contains elements of both. Second, an *epistemological* distinction between different kinds of knowledge: whatever we know, we either know through our senses or our mind, or through a combination of both. And, third, an *ethical* distinction with respect to what we value and, accordingly, how we live: we strive toward either material or ideal goods, or a mixture of the two. These distinctions, as most famously illustrated in the allegories of the cave, the line, and the sun in the *Republic*, are explicitly hierarchical. The soul exists in a substantially more profound way than the body (it is immortal while the body is not); thought leads us to truth while sensual knowledge leaves us only with appearances; and to live by cherishing what is morally good rather than what is materially valuable is the only way to real happiness.

Notwithstanding possible modifications of this stark three-dimensional dualism in other works by Plato (which some scholars may point at in order to defend Plato against charges from "postdualistic" thinkers) it is beyond doubt that, historically speaking, it had a profound influence on the further development of mainstream Western religion and philosophy ranging from Christianity (Saint Augustine and others) to Descartes and Spinoza, and then on to Kant and Hegel. One could write a whole series of books describing in detail how each of these thinkers integrated, criticized, sharpened, or softened the ontological, the epistemological, and the ethical aspects of the Platonic mind-body dualism. In many ways, Whitehead was entirely correct when he famously stated that European philosophy essentially kept itself busy with producing footnotes to Plato, or, more precisely, footnotes to Plato's triple distinction.

The attitude of the footnote writers changed considerably in the nineteenth century. With authors like Marx and Nietzsche, reactions to the triple dualism became much more hostile. With Hegel and Feuerbach, idealism had reached its highest forms of expression and was bound to decline. The old hierarchy (that had previously been challenged by some, for instance, Spinoza) is now attacked openly. The values are to be reevaluated. Hegel has to be turned from his head to his feet (by Marx), and Plato and Socrates have to be exposed as responsible for the decay of philosophy (by Nietzsche). It is, for Marx, material being that determines consciousness, and not the other way around. One of the great errors that plagued Western thought, as Nietzsche proclaims, was to confuse the relation between the physical and the spiritual. When we eat frugally, we may deceive ourselves that by our "free will" we impose a "diet" on our body. In fact, Nietzsche says, we only hide from ourselves the real causes and effects which are exactly vice versa: when we intellectually decide to go on a diet, we do so only because our body is already too sick to eat freely.[2]

Marx and Nietzsche, each in their own specific way, inverted Plato's threefold hierarchy. For Marx, what we *are* economically is more substantial than what we may be intellectually; to understand our material conditions is more fundamental than to understand the world spiritually. The real moral responsibility of the philosopher is to change the material world rather than to merely add another moralistic interpretation. For Nietzsche, our physiology characterizes us more than our mind; thus to know ourselves physiologically is more interesting than reflecting on our soul, and, perhaps most important for him, in order to overcome our traditional "slave morality" we have to honestly affirm our physiology rather than construct a system of values that nihilistically restricts the forces of life.

In the twentieth century, the reevaluation of Plato's triple dualism continues. Freud transforms Nietzsche's philosophy into a psychological theory and "scientifically" outlines how human existence, both individually and collectively, is founded on unconscious "drives," wishes, and anxieties that spring from our physiological being, that is, our sexuality and digestion. In philosophy, a phenomenology of life energies and the body becomes popular (Bergson, Merleau-Ponty). And later on, feminist and deconstructionist ideas are infused into the humanities and the social sciences, and, by focusing on gender issues, contribute to the demise of older "phallocentric" and "logocentric" hierarchies.

If, at least academically, the Platonic reign of the soul over the physical has been largely discredited, this does not mean that, philosophically speaking, the age-old mind-body problem has been solved. The traditional order has been thoroughly shattered and one can now choose between various ways of attributing ontological, epistemological, or ethical (non)priority to mind and body respectively. However, the old *vocabulary* along with its philosophical "grammar" (in the Wittgensteinian sense) still prevails. And this is not only academically true, but also in ordinary language. We can still use the word "brain" in such sentences as, "she is the brains behind Pa" or "use your brain!" It is still believed that brain science can actually find out how whatever happens physiologically in the brain determines what happens in our mind, that is, how we think and feel. Alternatively, we believe that many illnesses are psychosomatic. "Stress" leads to anxiety, and anxiety leads to bodily malfunctions. On the positive side, our mental attitude may allow us to win a sports competition. If we are appropriately motivated, we will perhaps outperform our physically advantaged opponent. The triple dualism is still both academically and in ordinary life a most essential commonsense ontological, epistemological, and ethical concept. While the dominance of the soul over the body is no longer an accepted theory, there is still something like a common consensus that the world is made up of the physical and the intellectual, that we can know things either through reflection or experience, and that we can act according to material or ideal values. In this sense, Plato's triple dualism is as alive as it ever was.

Modern Western philosophy succeeded in loosening the hierarchical and dynamic structure of the mind-body dualism, but it did not succeed in—or, probably more correctly, never had the intention of—replacing the model as such. Demands for integrating the mental and the physical into a psychosomatic continuum and for acknowledging the material as the basis for the ideal still operate well within the traditional mind-body semantics. They offer alternative and, in part, novel ways of arranging the concepts in relation to one another, but they stick to the traditional pattern of conceiving of ontological, epistemological, and ethical issues in mind-body terms.

This semantic continuity cannot but perpetuate what may be called the chronic discursive illness that has been labeled the mind-body *problem*. When Descartes, for instance, tried to answer how to practically follow his demand for overcoming the "passions of the soul" (i.e., a state in which the soul is passively subjected to an active body) and for exerting intellectual domination of the material, he was forced to somehow explain how one agency, namely *res cogitans*, can concretely exert its control over another and *substantially different* agency, namely *res extensa*. In other words, how can the mind actually "get in touch" with the body, or how can the body physically direct mental activity? Descartes came up with a daring hypothesis that nowadays seems rather curious; he maintained that the soul had "its principal seat in the little gland which exists in the middle of the brain" (the so-called pineal gland) and the power to move this gland in such a way that "animal spirits" could be emitted and sent to the various body parts (through the blood and nerves) in order to steer the "machine of the body."[3] However, as Descartes pointed out, a weak soul was not powerful enough to exert such control and thus the steering mechanism could also work in reverse. In the case of a weak soul, the body would be able to force the soul into passivity (the state of "passion") and control it by directing the motions of the pineal gland. In a state of "passionate" love or anger, for instance, our physical impulses are thus able to subdue our intellect.

Descartes's model is a simple form of a cybernetic mechanism, that is, a mechanism consisting of an active steering part and another part that is passively steered, just like a car. As long as we are fully conscious, we are able to impose on the car we are driving the direction that it has to take. If, however, we are drunk or fall asleep at the wheel, the steering relation is reversed and the car will take us with it and manipulate our movements. The mind-body (or consciousness/ matter) relations suggested by Nietzsche, Marx, and Freud may well be more complicated than Descartes's, but they are still at the level of mechanistic cybernetics. They are about various degrees of agency and passion, of being in control or being controlled. Similarly, most contemporary scientific and popular models of mind-body interaction will try to outline or predict the effects that certain physiological processes have on mental ones, or vice versa. Brain scientists produce research on what sort of brain activity produces what sort of emotional and cognitive effects; and some psychotherapists will instruct their clients on how to heal themselves through positive thinking or other cognitive therapies. The Cartesian hypothesis about the concrete interaction between the soul and the body is now obsolete, but interactionism as such remains a popular option for mind-body mechanics. Thus, the mind-body *problem* remains unresolved. There are a number of vague ideas about how the brain can practically steer the mind, or how the mind can steer the brain, or how both can steer one another psychosomatically, but there is not one commonly accepted theoretical replacement for the pineal gland. That such steering happens is commonly assumed, but still no one knows how it works.

In other words, most contemporary views on the relation between mind and body are simply "mop-up operations" working within the general Cartesian "paradigm"—to use Thomas Kuhn's terminology. Luhmann is one of those theoreticians who try to *radically* depart from, to again use Kuhn's terminology, this kind of "normal science." He is, I believe, able to provide a convincing solution to the mind-body problem, which mechanistic models derived from the traditional Platonic triple dualism have failed to do.

Luhmann's break with the "normal science" of the mind-body relation and his subsequent solution to the mind-body problem is twofold. First, he adds a third concept to the dualism, namely *communication* (or, society as the system of communication), and thus transforms the dualism into a "triadism," which could also be understood as a pluralism. Second, he explains how the relations between these three systemic realms can be conceived differently from the traditional mechanical steering conceptions. He replaces a mechanistic cybernetics of steering with the second-order cybernetics of *system/environment* configurations. I first discuss Luhmann's triadism/pluralism and then his second-order cybernetics.[4]

Triadism/Pluralism

Unlike Descartes, Luhmann considers the mind and body not substances but systems. The use of the term "system" already denotes a shift from an ontological to a functional perspective. Systems are processes, not static things. Luhmann's systemic triadism is concerned with operations, and not with what essentially is. A system is a functional entity that is operationally distinct from and so distinguishable from other systems. It is, so to speak, a sequence of events that connect with one another, that is, that go along with one another diachronically, synchronically, or both. Luhmann focuses on autopoietic and operationally closed systems. That a system is autopoietic means that it is not externally produced or constructed but instead produces, constructs, and perpetuates or reproduces itself. Its operational closure means that its operations can only connect with its own operations, but not with those of any other system.

An example of a biological or physical system, that is, a living system, is the human body. The human body includes subsystems, such as the visual system and the immune system, but subsystems are not to be confused with parts that constitute a whole.[5] All operations within living systems are life operations, such as biochemical processes, hormonal processes, neurological processes, and so on. Each system functions by continuing its own operations with further operations of the same kind. The immune system, for instance, continues to function by further immune reactions. It cannot continue to function by visual operations. The system's function cannot be taken over by the visual system, or vice versa. A system is not a body *part* or an organ that can be potentially replaced by a spare part. One cannot transplant an immune system. Nor can it be amputated like an arm or taken out like the appendix. The view of the body as a biological life-system including a number of subsystems is therefore substantially different from a mechanistic view of the body as a whole consisting of parts.

The operations of biological systems are not dictated, or steered, or produced from the outside by a "divine watchmaker." Any biological system is an effect of the evolution of life and not some ready-made machine. Systems change by evolving. Different forms of life, nonhuman life for instance, have evolved differently. Some living systems do not have visual systems, but this does not mean that they *lack* anything. They are no less alive, and no less able to function, reproduce, and come up with (nonvisual) cognition.

An example of a psychic system is the human mind. Mental operations are thoughts, feelings, emotions, and so on. A mental system is operationally closed in the sense that no mind can directly interfere with the operations of another mind. One cannot continue someone else's mental activities by thinking or feeling for him or her. It is also impossible to immediately think what someone else is thinking, or to feel what someone else is feeling. We can hear what others say, or see an expression of pain or joy on their face, but we cannot literally think or feel what they do. Psychic systems are autopoietic. Just like living systems, they are integrated into evolutionary processes and exposed to environmental "perturbations." However, they are not created or steered like a machine by any external agency.

Communication systems are social systems. In other words, society consists of communicative operations. Such operations can be performed as speech or writing, that is, through language, but also by a large number of other means, for instance through signs, gestures, and facial expressions, as well as through monetary payments, the assigning of grades, the issuing of documents, the production of images, the composition of music, or a kiss on the cheek. Social systems are operationally closed and autopoietic as well. Communication in the education system can only be continued with further communication of the same kind. If I no longer lecture during my lectures, but instead insist on only singing beautiful songs, I will be fired (after a while). Nor are social systems, contrary to some modern humanist narratives, man-made. The economy cannot be planned, and the legal system was not established as the result of an invention by some clever individuals on a specific day in history. Just like living systems and psychic systems, social systems, such as the law, the economy, and the mass media, emerge through evolutionary processes, and they are continually changing.

Autopoietic systems are not necessarily limited to the body, mind, and society. It can be imagined that there are or will be other types of operationally closed and autopoietic systems. In his later works, Luhmann repeatedly speculated, albeit without elaboration, about the possibility of, for instance, the emergence of novel autopoietic systems that may operate on the basis of computer technology.[6] So far, computers, like all other machines, operate allopoietically, and not autopoietically, meaning they are not operationally closed. They are not (yet) self-generating and self-reproducing, and it is possible to immediately interfere in their operations. For instance, I am pressing a key on a keyboard right now, which is how the text that you are reading is currently being produced. No brain, social system, or mind can be steered in the way I steer my computer while writing this text. Therefore a better candidate for a fourth category of systems would perhaps be a nonliving natural system, such as, the global climate.[7]

In theory, Luhmann acknowledges the possibility of replacing the mind-body dualism with an unlimited pluralism. Concretely and in the present, the knowledge of the existence of autopoietic systems is nevertheless limited to three: living systems, psychic systems, and communication systems.

The operational closure of the three types of systems excludes the possibility of mutual steering processes like those envisioned by Descartes with respect to body and soul. There is no pineal gland by which the operations of one system are mechanically connected with those of another. This guarantees, so to speak, the operational autonomy of each system, and thereby its functional difference. This *functional differentiation* replaces the substantial or *ontological differentiation* as conceived by Plato and Descartes. While the mind-body dualism was an ontological and/or substance dualism, the mind-body-communication triad is a functional triad. Instead of substantial distinctions, there are functional differences.

Even Marx, arguably the most profound social theorist of the nineteenth century, was incapable of expanding the traditional dualism and replacing it with a triadism/pluralism. He did not acknowledge that society is neither ideal nor material, but *social,* that is, a system not constituted by physical or mental operations but by communication.

Marx overturned Hegel's idealist dualism and replaced it with a materialist dogma. Material "being," for Marx, determined consciousness, and not the other way around. He distinguished the material aspects within society (such as land, goods, the means of production, money, capital, and property) from ideal aspects (such as values, ideologies, religious belief, class consciousness, and knowledge). This division, notwithstanding the inverted hierarchy, neatly followed the dualist models of the past by distinguishing between material (i.e., economic) and ideal (e.g., the law, religion, morality) forces that strive for control over one another.

Marx was unable to acknowledge an essential difference with respect to the functioning of the economy, between what may be called material and virtual aspects, or, in terms of systems theory, between society and its environment. Land, goods, and the means of production are in fact *not* social. They exist in the material environment of society. Money, capital, and property, on the contrary, *are* social; they are virtual social constructs, that is, they are communicative constructs, or, more precisely, economic constructs. Land, goods, and machines can well exist in a society that has no economy—in the sense that it does not communicate economically. Land, for instance, before the evolution of money, capital, and property, did not yet have economic meaning in the modern sense of the term "economy." It may well have been used to feed people and animals, but it was not yet "observed" in economic terms. Native Americans, for instance, often could not understand the social construct of "selling" land when confronted with European settlers who wanted them to do exactly this. In order to observe land economically, and to sell and buy it, there has to be an economic communication system within which the transaction of selling land becomes meaningful. The economic meaning of land is, once again, not an effect of the material qualities of the land, but of how its value is observed and thus socially constructed in the economy. In this sense, the economy is *not* material; it is social. Marx was unable to see the decisive difference between the economy as a virtual communication system and its material environment. The economy is a communication system that exists within the social environment, which is constituted by the law, politics, education, and so on, and the extrasocial environment of living and psychic systems, that is, bodies, trees, land, human thoughts, feelings, beliefs, and do on.

From a systemic perspective, Marx's analysis of capitalist economy had two basic flaws: (1) the failure to properly distinguish between what belongs to the functioning of the economy as a social system and what belongs to its nonsocial environment, and (2) the failure to go beyond the traditional cybernetic concept of a hierarchical steering relation between different systemic realms. Marx still assumed that one system, namely the economy, could determine and therefore mechanically steer all other aspects of society. The traditional Marxist vocabulary that distinguishes between a base structure (the economy) and a superstructure (all other systems) in society demonstrates the mechanistic architecture of this theory. Society is described as a simple machine consisting of two basic components, one being in control and the other being controlled. It may thus be said that, somewhat ironically, the dualist heritage prevented even a revolutionary theory like Marxism from developing truly radical alternatives to traditional Platonic conceptions of society.[8]

System-Environment Multiplicity: No Nexus!

In comparison with nineteenth- and twentieth-century social theory, recent developments in the theory of consciousness, both popular and scientific, depart more radically from a dualist Platonic ontology, but not necessarily from Cartesian mechanics. It is quite common for people to assume that our mental processes are subject to both biological *and* communicative influences. Our thoughts and feelings, it is believed, are somehow related not only to what happens in our brain but also to what we experience in our social life. It is also acknowledged that a malfunction of certain neurological transmitters in our brain may have strong effects on our psychic well-being as well as on our capabilities of going to work or living within a family. Perhaps, by allowing for a triad of physical, mental, and social phenomena, psychological common sense has developed in a more complex way and distanced itself from Platonic dualism more than our current sociological and political self-descriptions.

Psychological common sense seems to accept the concept of a functional differentiation between what happens, respectively, in our brains, in our minds, and in our social life. But another major obstacle that prevents a radical departure from the Cartesian model unfortunately remains.

Descartes explicitly calls the pineal gland the principal seat of the mind. This concept of a *location* of the mind within the body was and remains an obstacle for a systemic understanding of the relation between mind, body, and other systems. In ancient Greece and ancient China, the heart was believed to be the principal seat of human consciousness. In the contemporary world, the brain is ascribed this role—so that the image of a *physical* place of the mind still remains. Not only metaphorically, but literally the mind and the brain are often linguistically identified with one another.

The image of two distinct systems coupled by the physical mechanism of a seat is misleading. It implies a causal link between two otherwise separate realms, along with the idea of at least potential control.

When I am physically sitting in the driver's seat I can, by being linked to it through all kinds of mechanisms such as the steering wheel and the accelerator, control the motions of my car. I am not simply the environment of the car, like the street or the air; I am located within it and at its center. Similarly, one can imagine not only a dualist, but also triadic and pluralist mechanistic cybernetics. It can be imagined, as perhaps some brain scientists and psychiatrists do, that by manipulating certain mechanisms in the brain, it will be possible to steer mental processes. Or, as perhaps some behaviorists or psychotherapists may believe, we may be able to control mental process by making people act or speak in a certain way. To proceed from dualism to a systemic triadism or pluralism is therefore not yet sufficient for radically solving the mind-body problem. In order to do this, we must discard not only Platonic ontology, but also Cartesian mechanics.

Systems theory should more appropriately be called system-environment theory. For Luhmann, the system/environment distinction replaces the subject/object distinction and revolutionizes the classical epistemology that comes with it.[9] This has at least two important consequences: (1) the notion of "unilateral control" by an active subject over a passive object has to be replaced by the notion of mutual feedback effects between systems that form a "cybernetic circle,"[10] and (2) the notion of an objective external view on internally accessible subjects has to be replaced by the distinction between operations that belong to any given system and those that occur in its environment, which is constituted by other systems. The terms "system" and "environment" are mutually dependent. An environment does not exist objectively, but only in relation to a specific system, that is, "the" environment is never the environment as such, but a concrete environment for a concrete system. Similarly, a system cannot exist subjectively on its own as "the" system, but only within an environment. While a system operates autonomously, it is existentially inconceivable without, and therefore entirely dependent on, its environment.

I stress again that despite the fact that systems theory usually speaks of systems, for lack of a more precise vocabulary, as being "in" or "within" an environment, this should not be confused with the Cartesian idea of a principal seat. A system has no seat in its environment in the sense of a specific location, or, to give a probably all too simplistic example: a fish has no principal seat in the water. That a system is within an environment means that it functions while other systems function simultaneously. A more appropriate example than the fish in the water is the immune system. We can well say that the immune system is within the body, but this does not mean that it has any principal seat in the body. The immune system can only exist within the complex environment of the body—it cannot work without blood circulation, digestive processes, and respiratory activity all functioning simultaneously. There is, however, no pineal or other gland that serves as the nexus between the immune system and its bodily environment. The very concept of a nexus is what the system/environment distinction is no longer in need of. And it was precisely this problem of the nexus that Cartesian mind-body dualism was unable to convincingly solve.

Just as the immune system has no specific seat in the body, systems theory argues, the mind has none—neither in the heart, the brain, or anywhere else in the body. Neither does it have a seat in the family, in one's job, in one's religion, or anywhere else in society. The mind, if conceived of as a human being's mental system, has no seat whatsoever. It is, however, only able to function within the environment, or, if this should be a more acceptable term, the context of the simultaneous functioning of a great number of other biological and social systems. That the immune system does not have a seat in the body does not mean that it can exist outside of a bodily environment. The same is true for the mind as a nonbiological system. The search for a seat of the mind has been a phantom created by the mechanistic cybernetics inherent to the mind/body dualist tradition as exemplified by Descartes. Once one radically breaks with this tradition, the seat becomes a mere chimera.

Instead of a simplistic mind-body dualism, systems theory suggests a highly complex pluralism of simultaneously operating systems. Even the brain is not "one" system. There are, to my knowledge, a great number of functions that constitute brain activity, including electrical, hormonal, neural, chemical, blood circulatory, cellular functions, and so on. The brain is a very complex biological systemic arrangement of various systemic functions. Not only is there no nexus between the brain as a whole and the mind, but there are also no discernable "nexi" between the specific biological systems functioning in the brain or between those specific systems and the mind.

Our minds operate within both a bodily and a social environment. Language acquisition, cognitive development, emotional activity, and so on, all have a lot to do not only with what goes on in our bodies (including the brain), but also with our social experiences. Again, there is no principal seat of the mind in society or of society in the mind. There is no gland by which how we communicate in our family, at our jobs, or with our money enters into our mind, or vice versa.

Taking a psychopharmacological drug will have an effect on one's body. It will have an effect on how you think and feel, which will ultimately have an effect on how you talk and what you do in society. Similarly, communicating with a psychotherapist will have an effect on how you think and feel, and this will also have effects on your body and brain. Physical, social, and mental systems function simultaneously and constitute environments for one another.

Given the complexity and plurality of simultaneous system/environment relations and the absence of any mechanical nexus between them, the effects of what happens in one system on what happens in another are at the same time limited and unlimited. They are limited in the sense that, given the absence of a causal nexus, they are not precisely predictable. They are unlimited in the sense that the effects are likely to produce further effects on a number of other systems that they were not intended to have an effect on. The problems attached to the so-called side effects of, for instance, psychopharmacological medication may illustrate this. The notion of "side effects" is misleading because it suggests that taking a certain drug will have a particular mechanical effect via one's body (i.e., one's brain) on one's mind, as well as some other less central effects that somehow do not fully count as effects since they are merely "on the side." The distinction between central and side effects, however, is entirely arbitrary and merely a semantic gesture. The side effect is no less of an effect than the central effect. With respect to a computer keyboard, for instance, the repeated pressing of the y key has the effect that many y's appear on the screen and that, over time, the y printed on the keyboard becomes less visible.

One may distinguish between intended and unintended effects in this case, but not between side effect and central effect.

The inference (which may well be drawn by a naive reader of a medication package) that the anticipation of effects, both "central" and "side," can ever be complete is much more problematic. Even if the desired effect of a psychopharmacological medication should come about in the body (let's say a modification of certain chemical processes in the brain), it is very difficult to predict if this desired effect in the body will also produce the desired effect in the mind (let's say the disappearance of anxiety). And it is even more difficult to predict what an effect in one system of the body (brain chemistry) will have on other bodily functions (e.g., sexual performance capacity), particularly in the long run. Usually, previously unknown side effects of taking a drug only emerge after a certain period of regular consumption. Furthermore, it is impossible to predict how a drug's mental and physical effects will, in turn, affect one's social life. What will the effect be of both decreased anxiety and decreased sexual performance capacity on one's family life, on one's professional life, on one's attitude toward spending money? To add another dimension of system/environment relations, what happens simultaneously to the taking of the drug in other aspects of one's life is entirely uncontrollable. Maybe the patient has some yet undiagnosed cancer; maybe he catches the flu; maybe there will be a rise in taxes or a loss in the value of his property; maybe he will be promoted to a position that he feels unable to cope with; maybe he falls in love; or maybe no rain will fall for two weeks. Any of these events will resonate with the event of taking the drug, and vice versa. This is obviously not to say that taking such a drug has no effect or that it has bad effects, or that one should not take drugs. It is only to say that it is no more than a fiction to assume that taking a drug works in any way similar to the Cartesian model of the pineal gland mechanism. The human body does not work like a car. It is embedded in highly complex system/environment connections stretching over many different systemic realms.

Mental, physical, and social systems (and, perhaps, others) are integrated into complex system-environment relations that, in Luhmann's words, cut through causal connections.[11] Therefore, strictly speaking, taking a drug does not "cause" anything. In Luhmannian terminology, it "irritates" or "perturbs" a large number of bodily, mental, and social systemic processes. All these systemic processes incessantly produce mutual resonance. The world does not remain the same afterward, or at least this would be a very unlikely effect of the irritation or perturbation. The traditional notion of causality becomes highly problematic with respect to system-environment relations. Not entirely unlike Hume's famous reflections on causality with respect to the playing of billiards,[12] social systems theory looks at the cause-and-effect relation primarily as an ascription. Cause and effect are not objective categories but systemic constructs, which is obvious with respect to the dubious notion of a "side effect." Causes and effects that are observed are, like all other observations, dependent on the observing system and its means of observation. The effects of taking a medical drug will be observed differently by the doctor, the patient, the pharmacological company, the medical insurance company, and so on. There is no such thing as *the* effect as such. The effects on the doctor's professional reputation; the pharmaceutical company's balance sheet; the patient's digestive system, his mental well-being, his wife's sex life; and so on, are all effects. What they are depends on the observational capabilities with which the various systems perceiving the effects are equipped. None of the effects can be labeled the central or proper effect as opposed to side effects. Such an ascription depends entirely on what is classified as central and peripheral by an observer. Side effects, like root causes, are semantic or ideological constructs.

Medical professionals—just like meteorologists and business consultants—are therefore, perhaps unbeknownst to themselves, far more post-Platonic and post-Cartesian than most academic social theorists or philosophers. Instead of believing in mind-body dualisms and root causes, specialists in medicine have largely, due to the progress of statistics, abandoned simplistic dualist and cause-effect models. By extension, they have also abandoned the belief that they can take control of what they are professionally dealing with. Instead, they operate with *probabilities*. In North America, a doctor will often let you know the probability of success of a specific treatment; a meteorologist will tell you the probability of rain tomorrow; and a business consultant will inform you about the probable profit of a certain investment. This means that, implicitly, these people have quietly accepted the multiplicity of systems and the absence of a causal nexus between them—there is a chance that what they do will bring about some desired effects, that their projections will be more or less correct, but there is also a chance that they won't. These people are aware that the probabilities with which they are working are only probable probabilities. In this way, Luhmann's theory may be the last footnote to Plato, which many professionals in contemporary society, unlike we academic scholars, don't even need to read anymore.

Luhmann successfully dissolved the traditional mind-body triple dualism. First, instead of an ontological division between ideal and material existence, there is a distinction between at least three, and potentially many more, kinds of systemic functions. There are psychic systems, living systems, and social systems. They do not split the world into a hierarchical structure of being, but into a complex arrangement of system/environment relations without any particular order. Second, instead of the hierarchical epistemological division between two kinds of knowledge, there is a differentiation between types of observation. Systems are observing systems and have their own internal capabilities for producing knowledge or cognition of their environment and of themselves. There is no privileged observatory platform and knowledge does not grant the ability to come to unequivocal conclusions or predictions. Observations are equally dependent on their operational modes. Third, the ethical distinction between ideal and material values and the subsequent formulation of normative prescriptions is simply absent from systems theory. It is, at least in its Luhmannian form, non-ethical and amoral and does not ascribe moral superiority or inferiority to any specific kind of system. It does not, for instance, repeat the traditional moral imperative that the intellect ought to subdue the body.

SIX

ECOLOGICAL EVOLUTION
A CHALLENGE TO SOCIAL CREATIONISM

Relatively speaking, one of the less conspicuous radical aspects of Luhmann's theory is his application of the theory of evolution to sociology. This may seem a somewhat strange point to make, given that the theory of evolution is no longer considered all that scandalous, at least outside of North American fundamentalist Protestant circles. The same may be the case with respect to biology, but Luhmann's use of evolutionary theory for a theory of society is, I believe, quite provocative. Although Luhmann is not a social Darwinist and has little in common with Herbert Spencer, his evolutionary approach is nevertheless at odds with the dominant liberal and humanist views on society, which can often be understood historically as secularized successors of Christian ideas.[1] Luhmann's theory radically breaks with anthropocentric views of society, just as Darwin broke with the Christian idea of the human being as the "crown of creation."[2] Thus, Luhmann's radical evolutionary view of society (which was decisively shaped by the post-Darwinian evolutionary biologists Humberto Maturana and Francisco Varela) when viewed from mainstream humanist post-Christian social theory, has the potential to be as offensive as Darwin's biological theory once was.

Evolution, for Luhmann, emerges as the complex coevolution of system-environment relations. In Darwin's vocabulary, evolution is the evolution of species that constitute environments for one another. An ecosystem indicates the coexistence of a great variety of life-systems without a center or a general steering mechanism. Within an ecosystem, all subsystems coevolve. A change in one subsystem, let's say a change in the oxygen level of the water in a lake, "perturbs" the plants in the lake and triggers evolutionary changes in them. This also triggers evolutionary changes in the fish. These evolutionary changes will again have an effect on the chemistry of the water, and so on. All of these things happen simultaneously. Coevolution means there are permanent feedback mechanisms between a multiplicity of simultaneously evolving systems. Changes trigger changes that trigger changes and so on.

Such a basic evolutionary model contradicts the central idea of creationism, namely, the primacy of an external or initial act of creation or (intelligent) design. A coevolutionary ecosystem is self-generating and self-contained and not designed or based on any specific a priori input. The difference between a theory of evolution and creationism parallels the difference between a theory of immanence on the one side and theories of transcendence or transcendental theories on the other. While current social theories are no longer transcendent and commonly do not speak about divine origins of social phenomena, they are often *transcendental* theories, to use the Kantian term—and thus represent, so to speak, a kind of secular social creationism.

Unfortunately, in English academic language, the foundational Kantian distinction between *transzendent* and *transzendental* is mostly ignored and the terms "transcendent" and "transcendental" are often used synonymously or interchangeably. Kant, however, used the term *transzendental* in particular to distinguish his philosophy from previous transcendent metaphysics. For him, *transzendent* meant "beyond experience" (God, for instance, is *transzendent*), whereas *transzendental* referred to whatever precedes experience in the sense of being the (or a) "condition of the possibility of experience." *Transzendental* is what is a priori in this sense, namely what is prior to or "pure of" anything empirical. Many contemporary social theories are, though certainly not transcendent, still, in a post-Kantian sense, transcendental theories of society. As such, they are still essentially incompatible with a radical evolutionary theory of society that is radically immanent and leaves no room for any a priori social principles.

Modern and contemporary social theories, like those of Hobbes, Rousseau, Habermas, and Rawls, can be called "transcendental." They, at least hypothetically, think that society either is or should be founded on some sort of a priori mechanism or basis for intrasocial consensus such as a contract, a commitment to reason, or a definition of fairness. Society is assumed to have access to something that is not itself social but an a priori condition for society to function well. Society, according to these models, can only be enacted properly if it adheres to certain principles. These principles are most commonly believed to be civil principles, that is, they are related to specifically human characteristics such as human nature, free will, human rationality, human rights, and so on. In this way, these transcendental theories of society are also inherently humanist, or, more precisely, anthropocentric. Luhmann's theory of society, like Darwin's theory of evolution, is not.

One profound difference between creationism and a theory of evolution is the idea of a plan. Creation is not random or involuntary; it involves intentionality. It involves action and agency. This agency can be transcendent or transcendental. In the first case the agent is of divine nature, that is, a God; in the second, agency is this-worldly. Evolutionary theory, however, denies both sacred and secular agency. An ecosystem cannot intentionally evolve. It neither enacts God's will nor freely determines how to develop itself. Luhmann's social theory has been criticized, in precisely this context, as being "metabiological" by Habermas,[3] because it follows evolutionary biology in denying not only transcendent, but also transcendental agency and intentionality. This is what makes Luhmann as scandalous in social theory today as Darwin's theory was in the context of nineteenth-century biology. Humans are no longer capable of their own development, but are simply an element within highly complex system-environment entanglements. To take evolution seriously means to take the notion of environment seriously, and therefore to undermine the concepts of intentionality, planning, and free will. None of the post-Kantian transcendental and anthropocentric social theories can be truly ecological so long as they ascribe the capabilities of design and agency to a privileged species.

Conventional transcendental social theories are incompatible with radically ecological and evolutionary social theories such as Luhmann's. While many progressive and, to a certain extent, leftist (at least in their own view), social theoreticians, like Habermas, take great pains to come up with nonhierarchical or egalitarian visions of society that eliminate structures of domination, they cannot be classified as noncentrist thinkers. Typically, these theorists affirm the central role of politics (or the economy, or both together) in society. If society is, in a post-Kantian sense, to rationally determine its own future, then there has to be a central planning agency for directing this development. This agency, as is the case for Habermas, may well be supposed to be democratic, that is, collective, nonrepressive, and nonauthoritarian, but it nevertheless has to have some sort of social centrality. It must have some authority over law, the economy, education, religion, and so on in order to ensure that society progresses in the right way. Luhmann, the evolutionary theoretician, goes against such a centrist vision. Instead, he "develops a polycentric (and accordingly polycontextural) theory in an acentrically conceived world and society."[4]

An ecosystem has no center. Evolution does not follow any guidelines or directives given by any of its subsystems. Subsystems are not egalitarian or democratic in the sense that each system has a the right to make a contribution in determining where evolution goes. Subsystems may compete for survival, and, in the long run, most of them will simply dissolve since they cannot plan their own future or the future of the whole. There is no institution inherent in evolutionary processes that a system may appeal to, or, for instance, complain to that its extinction is unjust, unfair, or irrational. A social theory that takes evolution seriously will therefore not only disappoint, but most likely offend those social theorists who think that even if such institutions may not yet exist or may not yet be perfect, they should at least be aspired to. Evolutionary theory, however, does not allow for such aspirations.

Modern social theories rooted in the Enlightenment hope that society can elucidate itself in a twofold sense; it has the ability to see itself more clearly and gain, at least potentially, a more or less complete understanding of itself, and it can work toward making itself brighter, that is, happier and better in a moral or pragmatic way, or both. An evolutionary theory is, in a sense, a counter-Enlightenment theory, since it theoretically excludes both of these achievements. A thoroughly immanent ecosystem, be it biological, mental, or social, does not, so to speak, include its own light switch. As Luhmann pointed out regularly, an observing system can, paradoxically, often see only what it cannot see—and what others cannot see. It can detect the blind spots of other systems and thereby draw some conclusions about its own. A perfect illumination is theoretically impossible. Light and darkness, metaphorically speaking (and alluding to Daoism), constitute each other in an evolutionary context. The very condition of seeing something is not to see everything. The ability to observe, paradoxically, also implies limitations, and thus inabilities, of observation.

The partial blindness that comes with evolution also implies a certain ethical and pragmatic blindness. Since it is impossible to see everything, it is also impossible to see what is good for all. An ecosystem that cannot know itself and that cannot know its future also cannot know what it should ultimately hope for. How can today's species know what will be good for future species? A bright future for one species implies necessarily, according to Darwin's theory, a dark future for others. The application of such a view on social theory must be deeply disconcerting for any sociologist or philosopher who shares the Enlightenment vision of a self-illuminating society.

A major Enlightenment narrative immediately connected with the program of self-illumination was the belief in progress.[5] Enlightenment as a process of human self-illumination is, both cognitively and practically, quite necessarily, geared toward improvement. The natural sciences provide us with more knowledge; new technologies enhance our capacities and productivity, and increase our material well-being. The social sciences, it was hoped, would provide us with expertise in social engineering so that we would be able to rationalize and optimize our political and economical life. Education was consequently seen as the means to lead ourselves out of our "self-inflicted immaturity"—to use the famous Kantian expression. Thinkers like Hegel, Marx, and the French positivists (Comte and others) subsequently came up with some of the grand nineteenth-century descriptions of a historical march to the light—of inevitable progress toward greater human self-realization—in the double meaning of this term, that is, both epistemologically and existentially.

The nineteenth century has been qualified as the century of historicism. This not only indicates a focus on the inherent historicity and dynamics of life, but also a belief in the possibility of a science of history.[6] History could finally be understood by those who make it. Marx is probably the prime example for such an attempt to identify the laws of history which, in the past, had shaped social developments unbeknownst to those who actually constituted or performed them. It was believed that an adequate analysis of the historical movement would enable humankind to actually make history rather than simply be moved forward through it. Instead of merely interpreting history, a historically informed social science would enable us to enact change rather than be merely subjected to it. In this sense, liberation for Marx also meant historical liberation: rather than being determined and dominated by history, humankind would now be able to determine and dominate it. Progress came to mean not only a development toward a better state but also, and perhaps even more important, a self-conscious motion. Progress thus meant to deliberately and actively move forward, to go on, by one's own will and in the direction that one set out beforehand.

The Enlightenment narrative of historical progress was soon questioned. Nietzsche replaced history with genealogy. Nietzsche, as well as many of the leading theorists of the twentieth century who were substantially influenced by him (one may think of Freud and Foucault in particular), was less optimistic about the idea of progress. On the one hand, these thinkers fully acknowledged the idea that what we are is an effect of what we have been—*Wesen ist, was gewesen ist*, as Hegel succinctly put it.[7] On the other hand, they did not really share the belief in the possibility of rationally improving the course of history. Simply put, genealogy may be defined as history minus progress. To understand our heritage does not necessarily mean that we can change or control it. Genetic engineering may in fact, from the perspective of a genealogy, turn out to be as futile as attempts at social engineering. Just as it is highly questionable how *improved* genetically modified food actually is, it is questionable how much improvement was brought about by the experiments in transforming historical knowledge into social progress.

In this sense, Luhmann's theory of social evolution fundamentally differs both from the historicist social theories of the nineteenth century and from Darwin's biological theory of evolution. For Darwin, in line with his historicist contemporaries, biological evolution was a story of progress. Evolution meant "survival of the fittest," and to be fit, as in contemporary popular usage, connoted being good, or at least better than the unfit. Similarly, natural selection meant the selection of the better over the worse. Darwin explicitly pointed out how "immeasurably superior" natural selection was, compared with "man's feeble efforts" to perfect living organisms over time.[8] This meant, for Darwin, that nature was even more concerned with bringing about biological advancement than, let us say, human horse breeders. Given this focus on improvement through selection, Herbert Spencer's social theory has rightly been labeled "social Darwinism" since it also conceives of evolution as progress, as a development toward the better.

Luhmann is *not* a social Darwinist in this sense. Social evolution for him, like biological evolution for post-Darwinist biologists, is not to be automatically equated with social progress.[9] Functional differentiation is an effect of social evolution, but it is not in any general way "better" than stratified or segmentary differentiation. Evolution is not teleological. Its partial blindness does not allow it to take aim. Furthermore, the lack of a central force or a socially progressive element (such as, for Marx, the proletariat, with the Communist Party as its avant-garde) makes it impossible to anticipate any specific course that history may take.

Post-Darwinian ecological evolutionary theory, in both biology and sociology, is genealogical rather than historicist.[10] It tries to understand its "genes," or its inherent heritage, and does not continue the Enlightenment narrative of progress. It refrains from scientifically evaluating species according to their respective merits and does not rank social systems or social structures. This does not mean a postulation on the equality of all biological or social systems; it means refraining from constructing a narrative based on value judgments. Not making value judgments also means not proclaiming that all systems are equally valid.

For a post-Darwinian ecological evolutionary theory, be it biological or sociological, development is contingent rather than necessary.[11] But contingency is an ambiguous term. It means to exist despite other alternatives having been equally possible, and to come into existence as a result of previously existing conditions in the sense of being contingent upon. It implies, on the one hand, the coexistence of a plurality of options or alternatives without hierarchical order, and, on the other hand, a nonarbitrary connection between what is and what has been. That there are horses is a contingent result of biological evolution in the sense that the emergence of other species or the extinction of the horse species would have been equally thinkable, given the extreme variety of evolutionary possibilities at all times. But it also means that the current existence of the horse species can be traced genealogically to a very specific evolutionary development that actually took place. Luhmann often stresses the unlikelihood of whatever is actually brought into existence by evolution, given all of the innumerable developments that might have taken place instead. This takes nothing away from the important role that everything that did evolve has within evolution. That horses came into existence was not evolutionarily necessary. Now that there are horses, they influence further evolutionary developments and thereby limit evolutionary possibilities. That something like stocks and bonds came into existence in social reality was not historically necessary. However, now that there are stocks and bonds, further economic, and thus social, evolution is contingent upon their existence.

Luhmannian ecological genealogy combines historical awareness with nondogmatic pluralism. In an evolutionary context, the notion of contingency affirms both historical heritage and the openness to the future. It implies both a confirmation of the relevance of the actual and recognition of its aleatory character. Everything might have come about differently, but now that the die has been cast there is no going back. And the options for the way forward are, although not predetermined, relatively limited by what is now the case.

Historicist theoreticians of progress share, unlike evolutionary genealogists, some of the teleological fantasies of the secular creationists. If there is, at least potentially, a plan for the course of history, and if we can both know and guide, or at least accelerate, this course, then radical contingency is unacceptable. For creationists and historicists, the course of history has a specific and necessary meaning and not only a contingent sense.[12] That history has a meaning is to say that there is some thread that runs through it, that it somehow unfolds as a plan, that it has a discernable design and is therefore determined to lead somewhere. Evolutionary genealogy recognizes or observes that evolution makes sense, but this making of sense is an immanent evolutionary construct, a dynamic process of continual reinvention.

From a genealogical evolutionary process, development is neither a priori nor teleologically determined. "Sense," as a linguistic alternative to the term "meaning," is *made,* while something *has* a meaning. In an ecosystem consisting of complex system-environment relations, sense is not singular. The system does not have *a* meaning, nor does it have any intention of pursuing a certain direction. What makes sense for one species does not necessarily make sense for another, and the evolutionary direction that the development of one species or biological system takes does not correspond to the direction of other species or systems in its environment. Human beings, for instance, have on average become a lot taller in recent centuries. This does not imply that other species became taller as well, or that evolution is generally aimed at tallness. Nevertheless, I am sure that the increased height of human beings will have perturbed the various subsystems within the human body and triggered certain evolutionary developments that biologists might be able to trace and make sense of. While there is no general meaning of having gotten taller (e.g., approaching a perfect human height), this change will help biologists make sense of a number of evolutionary changes in the human body (e.g., in the muscular system). It can even help sociologists explain how sociological change occurs, such as the production of longer beds. While a social systems theorist might make sense of an increasing variety in furniture size, Marxists may detect the meaning of this development in an ever-expanding capitalist economy, and liberals may see it as an indication of the liberation of consumer choice.

Traditional historicist attempts to define the trajectory of historical progress are, from an evolutionary perspective, comparable to biological attempts to define the trajectory of "progress" in human height. Biologically, it is uncommon to conceive of increased human body height as advancement toward an evolutionary goal. The idea of improving and purifying the biological development of human life was in fact one of the sociobiological experiments infamously conducted in twentieth-century Europe. Such a biopolitical project is certainly not compatible with an ecological post-Darwinian view of evolution. Ecological evolutionary theory avoids evaluations of what is desirable and what is not. It does not identify a developmental direction and it certainly does not try to give advice on how to help evolution move forward. From an Enlightenment perspective, this attitude may be criticized as a lack of engagement, but so far the concrete results of attempts to help either biological or social evolution reach its respective goals a little quicker have not been without their problems.

If, as Habermas has done, one labels Luhmann's social theory as "metabiological," then it should also be added, in order to avoid misunderstandings, that this means "metaevolutionary" and not "metacreationist." While social theorists like Habermas worked on the unfinished "project of Enlightenment" and its secularized creationist ideals, Luhmann subscribed to a radically different paradigm, namely the paradigm of ecological evolution.

SEVEN

CONSTRUCTIVISM AS POSTMODERNIST REALISM
A TEACHING OF DIFFERENCES

Among the many radicalisms that Luhmann adorned himself with was that of radical constructivism.[1] Such a self-designation was, academically speaking, among the less contentious of Luhmann's many radicalisms, since radical constructivism had been embraced by others before him.[2] Luhmann made fun of this somewhat unnecessary amplification of the term "constructivism." He called it "the latest fashion in epistemology," probably because he felt uneasy allying himself with a trend, considering that once a radicalism becomes a fashion it is no longer particularly radical.[3] Luhmann apparently only wanted to paradoxically underline his own radicalism by rhetorically distancing himself from a relatively established and thus no longer radical intellectual movement. He might have tried to salvage his own radical originality by adopting radical constructivism only in an ironic way. What makes Luhmann's constructivism radical is its ability to perform some sort of self-overcoming. In the end, Luhmann's constructivism is so radical that it turns out to be a realism at the same time. Simply put, Luhmann's constructivism says that what a construction constructs is reality, or, the other way around, reality is what a construction is capable of constructing. Realism and constructivism do not oppose but imply one another. Their difference collapses and they are reconciled.

How is such reconciliation possible? Constructivism, as unambiguously implied in the very title of his most important essay on this topic, "Cognition as Construction," is for Luhmann an epistemology, and thus not an ontology. Realism, on the other hand, is an ontology that can peacefully coexist with a constructivist epistemology. That Luhmann's radical constructivism does not stand in the way of a realistic ontology is evident from Luhmann's pronouncement: "*Es gibt Systeme*" (there are systems).[4] This is one of the primary axioms of social systems theory. Notwithstanding this axiom, Luhmann was careful not to stress the ontological dimensions of his theory and instead focused on his theory of cognition. In fact, he believed that ontology, in the sense of a theoretical distinction between being and nonbeing, had become obsolete and was no longer of primary importance.[5]

In spite of Luhmann's terminological aversion to the old-European notion of ontology, it might be permissible to say that a statement such as "there are systems" is ontological insofar as it refers to scientific or theoretical objects of research and thus facts (*Sachverhalte* in German).[6] In nearly the same terms as the early Wittgenstein,[7] Luhmann defines reality, or that which *is*, as that which *is the case*. Luhmann's ontology is therefore a realistic ontology of what is observed as "being the case." Constructivism supplies the epistemological analysis of the mechanisms that are capable of coming up with observations that constitute reality. Thus, constructivism, to put it in Kantian terms, describes the "*conditions* of the possibility" of reality, and is, in this way, theoretically prior to ontology. What was theoretically most interesting for Luhmann was not to ontologically distinguish what is from what is not, but to outline the epistemological foundations for making such an ontological distinction in the first place.

In this context, Luhmann, unlike Kant (and Hegel), is nevertheless *not* an idealist.[8] Cognition, for Luhmann, is not to be equated with consciousness. Luhmann's epistemology is functionalist. It is not concerned with the substance, which may or may not have cognition. In other words, not only mental or spiritual systems have the capacity to observe. Living systems and social systems are observing systems as well, and there may well be many more modes of observation other than mental, biological, or communicative processes. Reality is an effect of observation, but observation is not *substantially* defined. For the (German) idealists, epistemology was ultimately an enquiry into a certain substance, *Vernuft* (reason) in Kant's *Critique*, and *Geist* (spirit) and *Bewusstsein* (consciousness) in Hegel's *Phenomenology*.[9] Luhmann's epistemology is not grounded in such "ideal" conceptions. Whereas Luhmann's ontology can be described as an outcome of his epistemology, the idealist's epistemologies can be described as outcomes of their ontologies.

The epigraph that Luhmann chose for the final outline of his general theory, *Die Gesellschaft der Gesellschaft*, is axiom 2, part 1, from Spinoza's *Ethics*: "Id quod per aliud non potest concipi, per se concipi debet" (that which cannot be conceived through something else must be conceived through itself).[10] It is likely, I believe, that Luhmann read this sentence as a proclamation of a constructivist epistemology. Given the absence of a transcendent or transcendental access to reality, whatever is real depends on constructive self-conception. There is no reality given from above, nor is there any a priori mechanism that reality necessarily results from. Luhmann's theory, like Spinoza's, is one of radical immanence, which means that the emergence of whatever is real, or "the case," is an effect of immanent construction. Reality, in order to become real, has to construct itself. The act of constructing reality is an act of cognitive observation. It is its "own achievement," or, in the German constructivist vocabulary, it is *Eigenleistung*.

Here, something else has to be stressed: unlike Kant, Hegel *and* Spinoza, Luhmann is not a metaphysician. He conceived of himself as a sociologist. Luhmann borrows cognitive constructivism, along with the theory of autopoiesis, from evolutionary biology and second-order cybernetics, that is, from relatively applied fields. For Luhmann, a constructivist self-conception of reality as a systemic "own-achievement" is, first and foremost, communicative or social. Luhmann's radical constructivism is a radical *social* constructivism. The "facts" (in his Wittgensteinian conception of reality) that his theory deals with are the *Eigenleistungen* of society. This is what the obscure title of *Die Gesellschaft der Gesellschaft*, which, literally translated, means *The Society of Society*, says: society, as the social reality in general, is an "own-achievement" of social construction, that is, of communication as a form of observing or of cognition by making distinctions. Just as the reality of color vision emerges as an effect of the ability to cognitively distinguish colors, and thus can be described as the color-vision of color-vision, the reality of a distinct society emerges as an effect of communicative distinctions, and thus can be described as the society of society.

If the reality of society is an effect of social construction, then the descriptions of these constructions are also *immanent* social constructions. Luhmann's immanent epistemology results in an immanent ontology. Socially constructed realities, including the theories that describe these realities, are intrasocial phenomena. As opposed to either a transcendent idealist or a transcendental idealist, a radical epistemological constructivism is able to conceive of itself as well as of all the normative and evaluative standards in society as "society's own achievements instead of assuming that they are regulative ideas or components of the concept of communication."[11]

Luhmann's social constructivism is radical not despite but because it is a realism at the same time. Luhmann's constructivist realism does not deny the social reality of such ideas as free will, human rationality, or human rights. However, unlike social theory from Kant to Habermas and Rawls, it states that their very reality is an immanent effect of contingent social construction. This excludes the possibility of accusing radical constructivism of denying the reality of the real. It does not. It only states that the cognition of reality is, so to speak, the "real reality." In other words, when concepts such as general will, human rights, or a rationality of understanding come to the fore, they do so not because the things these terms are supposed to designate constitute a social reality, but because the discourses using such a language do.[12]

The descriptive analysis of society is itself an effect of what is described and does not have access to any a priori social normative or evaluative standards. Or, as Luhmann chose to express it: "In this way, the epistemologist becomes him/herself a rat in the labyrinth and has to reflect on the position from which he/she observes the other rats."[13] This is, to stay within Luhmann's image, not to deny the reality of the rats, but to acknowledge the fact that the observation of rats is itself a rather unusual social phenomenon, which can in turn be observed, just as the rats can. The radical constructivist observes the observer and thereby, autologically, posits some sort of labyrinth of immanence (or a "plane of immanence" to use Deleuze's expression.)

Theorists like Kant and Habermas look at the rats in the labyrinth believing that they are thereby looking transcendentally at reality or phenomena. Luhmann reflects on the strange fact that he is observing rats and that this constitutes the social reality of which one is a part and which needs to be explained as its "own-achievement." What has to be explained are not so much the rats, but rather the strange reality that someone is looking at rats in order to discover reality there. In more technical language, Luhmann describes this "autological" constructivist epistemological thusly: "Regardless of how cognition reflects on itself, the primary reality lies not in 'the world out there', but rather in the cognitive operations themselves." Once more, to avoid misunderstandings: for Luhmann, the social theorist, these cognitive operations in society are communications or discourses. Luhmann summarized his ontology even more succinctly when he said, "*Reality* is produced within the system by means of sense-making."[14]

A specific peculiarity of a realist ontology based on constructivist "sense-making" is that it, unlike most classical (Parmenidean, Platonic, and post-Platonic) "dialectical" ontologies (i.e., those that tried to arrive, simply put, at a "synthesis"), no longer assumes that reality is ultimately one, singular, or self-identical. Luhmann's ontology, I believe, can be classified as "postmodernist" precisely because of this break with the traditional philosophical preference of the one over the many. Like Derrida, Luhmann is a theoretician of differentiation rather than identification.[15] In a telling footnote at the beginning of *Social Systems*, Luhmann says (with regard to his usage of the identity/difference distinction): "An attentive reader will notice that we are discussing the difference between identity and difference, and not their identity. This is where the following reflections diverge from the dialectical tradition—despite similarities that may be noticed from time to time."[16] A whole book has been written on this issue. It tries to answer the question of which theoretical consequences result from Luhmann's shift from a primacy of identity to a primacy of difference.[17]

Interestingly enough (at least for me), this simple reevaluation of the identity-difference distinction can be traced back to Wittgenstein (just as Luhmann's usage of the term *Sachverhalte* as a basic ontological concept can). In his biography of Wittgenstein, Ray Monk mentions a conversation between Wittgenstein and Maurice Drury, his physician, that took place in Dublin in 1948 or 1949. According to Drury's recollection, Drury said something like: "Hegel seems to me to be always wanting to say that things which look different are really the same." Wittgenstein is reported to have replied: "Whereas my interest is in showing that things which look the same are really different." Ray Monk then adds that Wittgenstein "was thinking of using as a motto for his book [*Philosophical Investigations*] the Earl of Kent's phrase from *King Lear* (Act I, scene iv): 'I'll teach you differences.'"[18]

For Luhmann (just as, perhaps, for Wittgenstein), the construction of reality begins with the construction of difference. The "unmarked space" has to be violated in order for reality to emerge. "Draw a distinction!" is a dictum coined by the mathematician George Spencer Brown frequently quoted by Luhmann. For Luhmann, unlike for the "dialectical tradition," the difference established by drawing an epistemological distinction remains ontologically prior. In effect, this results in an ontology of radical differentiation. Simply put, reality is irreducible to any form of identity. It is, so to speak, hopelessly pluralistic. If reality emerges as an effect of contingent modes of cognitive observation, then it emerges in multiple ways that are incommensurable with one another. Luhmann's constructivist epistemology therefore leads to an ontology of multiple realities (but not multiple worlds).

With respect to social theory, Luhmann's insistence on the irreducible primacy of difference leads to a conception of multiple simultaneous social realities. On the one hand, each social system is capable of constructing a social reality as its "own-achievement." Unlike in unified social visions, such as that of Socrates in the *Republic* or Habermas's discourse community, society is not based on integrating ideas (such as goodness or justice) or norms stemming from general rationality. Luhmann speaks of the "dissolution of systems rationality" in modern society:[19] every social system, in Luhmann's terms, produces its own systemic rationality, and there is no lowest common denominator that unifies them. Luhmann maintains that his view on modern society "can be condensed into a difference-theoretical concept of systems rationality."[20] But, it may be asked, just how rational, in the Enlightenment-sense of this term from Kant to Habermas, is such a "difference-theoretical" multiple rationality?

When a society based on functional differentiation emerges, varieties of rationalities emerge and evolve. Legal rationality differs from political rationality, and political rationality differs from economic rationality, and so on. In a coevolutionary systems-environment context, all of these rationalities are continually changing. Along with these incommensurable rationalities, incommensurable realities emerge and evolve. The legal reality differs from that of politics or the economy. All these realities are subject to ceaseless change. Just as reality looks and feels different, and has different effects on different organisms within a specific ecosystem—and thus *is* different for every different organism included in it (the reality of a lake is radically different for the plants living in it than it is for the fish living there)—social reality *is* different for each social subsystem, including academic and scientific theories of society. The reality of society that emerges from a scientific or theoretical self-description of society is not "the" social reality, but one more in addition to those that already exist. By theoretically reducing social complexity in the form of a coherent social theory, social reality inevitably increases in complexity since another social construct has been achieved—just as attempts to de-complexify administrative structures by creating administrative units for administrative de-complexification will inevitably increase real administrative complexity.

To give a concrete example from the science system: I am writing this text on Luhmann in order to clarify his theory and to come up with a comprehensive interpretation that is supposed to unify its understanding and bring about consensus with respect to its meaning, value, and consequences. In effect, however, once this text is published, it will—if academically and thus socially successful—in turn be interpreted, thus increasing the complexities with respect to the reception of Luhmann's theory. In order for it to be socially successful, it must, therefore, paradoxically, but inevitably, miss its goal and *not* achieve consensus.

Or, to give another similar example: Kant's *Prolegomena to any Future Metaphysics That Will Be Able to Present Itself as Science* was metaphysically (as an academic book on metaphysics, and thus as social communication) successful only because of and not despite its complete failure to be what its title promised. The publication of this treatise did not mark the beginning of a "future metaphysics that will be able to present itself as science," but, to the contrary, the end of such presumptuous metaphysical attempts. After this treatise, the history, or more precisely, the genealogy, of scientific metaphysics could be written. That was its major effect. To speak in Hegelian terms, it functioned according to the logic of the inverted or topsy-turvy world (*verkehrte Welt*).[21] Rather than determining the future development of metaphysics by providing it with a foundational grounding, Kant joined the ship of fools of metaphysicians and made it possible to look at the reality of metaphysics as a curious episode within the evolution of modern society. Instead of being the founder of a new science, Kant could be considered a philosopher who made the foolishness of the endeavor of a *Prolegomena for Any Future Metaphysics* finally obvious. Kant, like Habermas and others who followed in his footsteps, failed to understand this "social ontology." Reality, by being observed, described, and analyzed, becomes further complicated than it had been before it was observed.

Accidentally, we may now have reached one of the "similarities that may be noticed from time to time" with the "dialectical tradition," or, more precisely, with Hegel. If Donald Phillip Verene is correct, Hegel's concept of the topsy-turvy world was borrowed from a play of that title by Ludwig Tieck, a contemporary of Hegel and a leading German romantic author. This play, in turn, is related to a much earlier work of German literature, the *Narrenschiff* (Ship of Fools) by Sebastian Brant (1494).[22] According to Verene's reading, Hegel's concept of the topsy-turvy world was, given these connections, intended to be ironic and was meant to expose the grotesque self-contradictions and self-refutations within the scientific philosophies of Kant and others. By attempting to define the order of reality, such philosophies only further confused it.

Just as Verene, via Tieck and the *Ship of Fools*, discovers a level of irony in Hegel's treatment of the history of philosophy in the *Phenomenology*, one cannot but discover a level of irony in Luhmann's realist ontology. Given that reality is incommensurably plural, and any observation of reality only adds to this plurality, an ontology necessarily contains some degree of self-refutation. Insofar as Luhmann's ontology is complete, it is, paradoxically, incomplete. Unlike Kant's ontology (and that of social theorists like Habermas), Luhmann's ontology (and perhaps Hegel's, if one follows Verene's interpretation) is ironical. Its wisdom consists, at least in part, in consciously demonstrating its paradoxical limitations and contradictions. An ontology based on difference rather than identity is bound to imply the possibility of different ontologies and thus necessarily includes a proof of its own contingency. While Kant's *Prolegomena* represents a serious attempt to determine reality and to rid it of its paradoxes, Luhmann's theory attempts to prove why such attempts, including his own, are inherently paradoxical.

However, just as I think that Luhmann's constructivist realism does not lack in realism only because it is constructivist, I do not think that his postmodernist pluralist realism is less realist only because it is pluralist. Similarly, I would oppose accusations that it is not fully realist only because it is ironic or paradoxical. To the contrary, I think that a realism that is capable of fully accounting for a radically pluralist and paradoxical reality may be more realist than traditional ontologies. To reiterate the ironic Hegelian theme of the topsy-turvy world: if reality actually is topsy-turvy, then an ontology that is able to account for this topsy-turviness may well be more realist than one that pretends to be capable of straightening it out.

To conclude these reflections on Luhmann's ontology of difference, I return once more to Wittgenstein. In his *Tractatus*, Wittgenstein had conceived of reality (or "the world") as the sum of all facts that are "the case." Reality, therefore, does not consist of things, but of effects of observation. For the early Wittgenstein, the mode of observation that would allow for the establishment of whatever is the case was language, and, in particular, a purified and logically correct and coherent language. In his later works, however, Wittgenstein admitted "severe errors" in his earlier approach.[23] Instead of looking to establish an artificially purified, logically coherent language that would provide us with the possibility to see clearly that "which is the case," and thus establish a similarly coherent world or reality, Wittgenstein was now concerned with "ordinary language." He came to accept the fact that real language is not necessarily coherent or pure. The artificial "language game" of the *Tractatus* did not clarify the facts, but simply constituted another way of doing philosophy by adding another text to the world. The later Wittgenstein denounced his earlier obsession with linguistic purity as a means for delineating the real world and shifted toward a preoccupation with the often incoherent and incommensurable differences that exist in language. This is, I suppose, why he intended to choose "I'll teach you differences" as a motto.

At one point in *Philosophical Investigations*, Wittgenstein metaphorically accuses himself of having gotten on to "slippery ice," onto a surface that is too smooth for people to walk on. He urges himself to return: "Back on to the rough ground!"[24] If I understand it correctly, what Wittgenstein is saying is: back on to the rough ground of "ordinary language." And thus away from the all too smooth and slippery ground of the artificially purified language that the *Tractatus* had envisioned. Wittgenstein was ready to shift from a language philosophy based on logical coherence and identity to one of difference and plurality. Language and that which is the case, and thus the world or reality, is not smooth; it is a "rough ground."

Luhmann was not a language philosopher. He was a social theorist, which for him meant a theorist of communication. Language is only one of the means by which communication can operate. Nevertheless, for Luhmann, real or ordinary communication was "rough ground" as well. Unlike for Habermas, for Luhmann it made no sense to try and smooth it out so that it becomes an even surface. Wittgenstein said that, in a certain way, a perfectly smooth and icy surface could be called an ideal ground—but it is also a ground that one cannot walk on.[25] If I am not mistaken, Luhmann's constructivist ontology of a social reality based on difference rather than identity opposes attempts by traditional "rationalist" theoreticians like Kant and Habermas to "smooth" society, communication, and reality. Such a seemingly ideal society, he was afraid, might be too *unreal* to be inhabitable.

EIGHT

DEMOCRACY AS A UTOPIA
A DECONSTRUCTION OF POLITICS

While Luhmann did not believe that democracy exists in the sense of "rule of the people," he did not deny that there is a mode of government in contemporary society that is named "democratic" and that this term usually refers to a "specific structural arrangement" of the political system.[1] That is to say, for Luhmann, democracy is not a term that should be discarded. It indeed says something, just not what it actually means. While the idea of democracy seems quite unfit to describe the functioning of politics in today's world, the term nevertheless signifies a specific way of doing politics. But what exactly does it signify, if not the rule of the people? What is, sociologically speaking, "actually existing democracy"? I suggest that Luhmann's answer to this question can be divided into three parts: First, being a type of politics, democracy denotes a form of exercising power, or more precisely, of establishing "collectively binding decisions" in society. Second, and more specifically, it denotes a political structure that allows for a continual alternation between government and opposition and thus manages to provide the political system with a balance of stability and variety that has proven successful in the sense of maintaining systemic durability. Third, it denotes a symbolism that provides the political system with what it needs most in order to be able to fulfill its social function of establishing collectively binding decisions in a durable way, namely, it denotes legitimacy.

Political power, according to Luhmann, is the power to make collectively binding decisions. This power typically rests with the government. These decisions may concern anything in society, ranging from regulations on what to wear (on your head, for instance), to what is taught in schools, right up to a proposal to fly to the moon. Such decisions express a specific political will and are made by governments that are authorized to express and enforce this will. Such a definition of politics, including democratic politics, is not radical but rather commonsensical. However, in the context of social systems theory, and in connection with a theory of functional differentiation, it leads to some rather paradoxical conclusions, namely that political power is not very powerful and that political decisions do not decide much.

I discuss these two consequences by referring to two examples of political decision-making in areas that have been fairly relevant (not only) in current democracies, namely governmental regulations and warfare. The power to regulate public institutions—even if they function within other systems—rests with the political system. It can politically regulate universities and hospitals, the legal system, or even the economy by, for instance, supporting private banks or other companies. Nevertheless, at least under democratic conditions, the power to regulate simultaneously leads to the creation of other nonpolitical powers—by politically regulating the education system, the military, or the economy, these very systems are then empowered to function on their own terms. The exercise of political power is not a zero-sum game; it does not absorb all social power, but enforces a dynamic social power structure. Hospitals, for instance, and not the government, have the power to declare people insane or sane; schools have the power to let people graduate or not; courts have the power to declare people guilty or innocent; and the economy has the power to make people rich or poor. These powers are not immediate political powers. Under the conditions of functional differentiation the power of establishing collectively binding decisions within the political system is necessarily limited by the complex social powers exerted by its intrasocial and extrasocial environment. It is limited, for instance, not only by the powers of law and science, but also by the powers of nature (such as, for

DEMOCRACY AS A UTOPIA

instance, by the fact that the oil reserves are not inexhaustible). Under the conditions of functional differentiation, that is, the coexistence of a number of autopoietic social subsystems, there is no social center and thus also no absolute power center in society. The diffusion of power does not simply follow a center-periphery structure (which is *not* to say that there are no center-periphery power structures at all) but a highly complex assemblage of power feedback mechanisms. Political power simultaneously regulates and is regulated by, limits and is limited by, legal power, economic power, media power, and so on.

Similarly, the power of the political system to make important decisions, for instance the decision to go to war, should not be confused with the power to determine what happens after the decision has been made. The power to declare war or not obviously does not translate into the power to decide who wins the war or even to end the war when one wishes to. Under the conditions of functional differentiation, the number of decisive social factors cannot be controlled. A political decision to go to war only necessitates further political decisions that will in one way or another react to decisions made by other systems, such as, once again, the economy, the media, the legal system, and so on. Just as the political system has no power monopoly in society, it has no monopoly on decisions. It has a monopoly on making political decisions and for exercising political power, but these monopolies exist in the context of ongoing and simultaneous decision-making and the exercise of power by other systems. In this sense, political decisions ultimately decide or determine nothing (and neither do those of any other system), they only enable the political system to make further decisions. Once the troops are sent to another country, other decisions must (and can and will be) made, such as what they will do there? how long will they stay? will troop numbers be increased or reduced, and so on.[2] Obviously, all these decisions will, in turn, make it necessary for the political system to generate further decisions.

An example of the powerless power of the political system and its inability to come to decisive decisions is the present issue of global warming. There is significant demand for political decisions that are supposed to help or even stop climate change. But how can the political system "control" the climate? The outcome of a war on global warming is no more predictable than the outcome of a war on terror or a war on drugs. The media system, the economy, the legal system, and, obviously, the extrasocial environment ("heaven and earth," as the Chinese used to say), do not and cannot stop exercising their own powers and making their own decisions once the political system has made its. There is no doubt that the political system can and does exercise its powers and make collectively binding decisions with respect to climate change, but it is quite inconceivable that the political system might determine the outcome of these decisions. If the political system were able to make final decisions, it would, paradoxically, undermine its very function in society. If a political decision were final, there would be no need for further political decisions and thus politics would become obsolete. Final decision-making would be the end of politics—particularly in an actually existing democracy. This is not to say that the political system is entirely powerless or entirely nondecisive, but its powers and decisions are not and cannot be privileged within society and the world.

Collectively binding decisions can be made and political power can be exercised by different political systems, both nondemocratic and democratic. However, it seems that, on the whole, democratic countries have achieved grander success than others in two important respects: they seem to be superior, at least at present, in establishing stable and durable political structures, and they seem superior insofar as they are commonly (which, nowadays, typically means in the mass media system) perceived to be legitimate.

Expressed in the terminology that Luhmann uses in his analysis of the mass media system, it may well be said that the democratic process produces a "stabilization of a relationship of redundancy and variety."[3] Democracy produces stability by allowing a certain degree of instability: governments change, but the system thereby remains intact. This kind of stability could also be called "stability by flexibility"—a kind of stability like that of an airplane wing, which does not break because it is not too rigid. Similarly, one could conceive of economic stability as being based on flexibility. In the capitalist economy, for instance, prices are not stable. Economies that are able to tolerate a certain flexibility in prices and operate with moderate inflation have proven to be more durable than economies that have tried to eliminate inflation altogether, as was unsuccessfully attempted in some Communist countries.

The code that allows for the "stabilization of a relationship of redundancy and variety" in the political system is the distinction between government and opposition. In general elections, our current democracies have established a mechanism that allows for regular alternations of these roles so that those in government and those in opposition frequently (but not too frequently) trade places. On the one hand, there are normally at least two organizations, that is, parties, or candidates, who are seriously competing for power. On the other hand, the individual parties, and even the political personages, tend to remain stable over an extended period of time. We get, so to speak, the best of two worlds: things change, so that the impression that something is happening and that development takes place can be upheld, while there is also a nonchaotic multiplicity of political organizations and drastic differences of ideology, and so there is no need for reorienting ourselves on a daily basis.

In the past, there have been democracies that collapsed due to an overdose of variety. One can think of the period between the two world wars in Germany. The political system of the Weimar Republic suffered from open hostilities between ideological camps (liberals, conservatives, socialists, communists, and fascists) that tended to fight for ultimate supremacy rather than agreeing to coexist. The strong ideological identity of each of the various parties did not favor moderate approaches to politics. In a way, the seriousness of the political parties, their commitment to their respective ideologies, created a spectrum of political variety that turned the political arena into a battlefield and made it impossible for the political system to fulfill its primary function, namely, to make collectively binding decisions. Today, the difficulties that are encountered in trying to establish a democratic political system in countries like Iraq or Afghanistan may also be related to the present struggle to reduce variety. If multiple political forces that represent mutually hostile ideologies, ethnicities, or religious groups compete for power, then political variety may increase to a degree that eliminates all political redundancy. If who governs and who does not is literally of vital importance for all political forces—if it is a matter of life and death—then the very strife for being in government may easily lead to a breakdown of the political system. Paradoxically, a functioning democratic system seems to be based on a good dose of redundancy. It seems that as long as politics are relatively redundant, democracy thrives—as long as no one *really* cares who governs today, because things may be different (but not too different) as soon as tomorrow. Even a chaotic political landscape, with a great number of political parties and frequent changes between government and opposition—as in Italy—can remain remarkably stable so long as this chaos remains redundant and is not taken too seriously.

On the other hand, a lack of variety may also threaten a democracy and thus political stability. Governments of countries that called themselves democratic but operated factually on the basis of a single-party system typically ended up with tremendous difficulties in legitimizing themselves. A total lack of variety, the seemingly endless continuation of the government, and, in some cases, the suppression of any meaningful opposition lead to a situation in which the political system must pay for its ability to *enforce* collectively binding decisions by not only losing its perceived legitimacy, but also by the breakdown of functioning couplings with other social systems. The ruling party effectively functioned as a self-serving organization that hijacked the political system for its own self-interest. And other social systems, such as the economy, the law, the media, were unable to develop independently. The economy was supposed to fulfill a political dream, namely equality; the law was supposed to deliver political justice; science was supposed to prove the truth of the political ideology, and so on. Functional differentiation did not function well in these societies. None of the goals were realized. Instead, one organization, the ruling party, had become a parasite on all social systems—and had taken over not only politics, but also the economy, law, science—and, unsuccessfully, tried to steer these. What actually happened was not a steering and controlling of society by politics, but a quixotic fight against the windmills of functional differentiation on the scale of a world society that led to a more or less complete social breakdown.

The basic code that underlies democratic politics is the distinction between government and opposition. It seems that the stability of democratic politics correlates with a "stabilization of a relationship of redundancy and variety"—in particular with respect to the government/opposition distinction. There is no general principle or ratio that would define, once and for all, the specific degrees of redundancy and variety that lead to stability. However, the elimination of one of these two elements seems to present a serious danger to any specific political system. Democracies have developed a highly effective social mechanism for maintaining this stability: periodical elections.

General elections allow for both the determining and the concrete distinction between government and opposition in a democracy for a certain time—and thus redundancy—as well as for the possibility of variety, namely the exchange of roles between the government and the opposition. Perhaps even more important, with respect to the stabilization of the political system, is that they also produce what Luhmann calls a "reflexivity of power relations" (*Reflexivwerden der Machtverhältnisse*) by, as he puts it, the "inclusion of the audience into the differing-out of the political system."[4] This rather awkward formulation essentially means that through general and free elections the audience (or the public) becomes a factor in both distributing and legitimizing political power; it takes part in establishing both redundancy and variety. The audience is, of course, the electorate. In an election, the voters, who are otherwise restricted to the passive role of observing, are activated, and do indeed, according to strictly regulated processes and rules, contribute to the delegation of political functions. The specific rules of elections vary from state to state and country to country (how the votes are counted, who is eligible to vote, how many votes a voter has, how frequent elections are to take place, which political functions are distributed through elections, how candidates are nominated, etc.) and thus are, to a significant degree, contingent, arbitrary, and subject to change. There is no specific formula that would rationally or logically translate any given election result into a "correct" distribution of political positions and power. There are democratically elected presidents who have received significantly less votes than their opponents. There are democratically elected presidents whose number of votes was less than 20 percent of the overall electorate. There are parties participating in governments who only received about 5 percent of the popular vote while others who received more than 30 percent are in the opposition, and so on. None of these cases are exceptions, but are in fact rather common. This is perhaps why Luhmann calls the election process a periodic invitation to the electorate to "cast dice."[5]

The electorate produces certain relations of numbers that, according to the respective rules of the election, may result, for instance, in a certain number of seats in Parliament for certain parties. Voters typically have little knowledge about the individual representatives actually sitting in Parliament (only a few voters will be able to name more than a handful) and have no power to control the actual political decisions of these representatives in between elections. There is also no correlation between whatever intentions individual voters have when they cast ballots and the concrete political effects of the numerical results of the election. It is likely that not a single voter intended the particular distribution of parliamentary seats and governmental positions or the particular set of political decisions that follow an election. This is why an election is, in Luhmann's view, not much less random than throwing dice. If an election were to be repeated a week later, let's say for some technical reason, the results would certainly be different even though the world would hardly have changed. The democratic election process includes the audience in the process of distributing political power, but it does this in a highly contingent way. In other words, what the political system does with the numbers generated by an election is up to the political system itself. It is up to the system, according to its own respective rules and procedures, to interpret the numbers politically. Once the numbers have been generated, only the political system, not the electorate, can transform the numbers into political decisions.

Empirically speaking, the democratic election process is not only a random procedure, it is also not really a (and much less *the*) central factor in the making of democratic politics. In the words of Edwin Czerwick, Luhmann distinguishes between the official (but mostly imaginary) narrative about the "circle of power" and its unofficial but actual circle: "According to the official circle of power, the audience determines through elections the persons that are to become the parliamentary representatives and then elect the government. The government makes the decisions—along with the Parliament and the administration—that the administration then implements and that concern the audience. Within the unofficial circle of power—which, according to Luhmann, is the rule—the public administration prepares the decisions on which the governments and the parliaments then bindingly decide and then justify their decisions to the audience. The audience then reacts with either approval or disapproval."[6]

The decisive difference between Luhmann's analysis of democracy and the common understanding of its "official circle of power" is that, for him, the voters do not represent the people as the source of all political power. They merely constitute the periodically activated audience of the political system which, by this very activity, is integrated into a circle of political decision-making. An election is not constitutive of political power; it is just one element within an ongoing political process. Actually existing democracies are not run by the people and their elections, but are "specific structural arrangements" of a number of political organizations, procedures, and institutions that enable themselves to remain relatively stable by, for instance, allowing for a smooth and often relatively inconsequential change between government and opposition. As soon as the election is lost, the opposition can begin preparing for the next one.

Under these circumstances, the role of the people is primarily (but not "merely") symbolic, or, in other words, the democratic narrative is a myth that serves the function of closing the political circle described above. Luhmann explains that in a democracy based on the government/opposition distinction, the people are only needed as the unitary formula for alternating differences: "As in the 18th century, the people is only a construct by which political theory accomplishes closure. Or, put differently: Who would notice it if there would be no people at all?"[7] The people, as a unit, is a fiction produced by the quasi-magical event of the election process. It is, so to speak, much more a mathematical effect than anything else. The election generates a single result, a single "will of the people"—to which the politicians unequivocally refer and from which they derive their legitimacy. Empirically speaking, however, it would be difficult to identify this will of the people with the will of any given individual. It is not really the people that are needed for a functioning democracy, but the symbolical construct of a numerical relation that is generated by an election.

Luhmann sarcastically alludes to religious beliefs when he says: "In the text of its self-description, democracy still presupposes the 'people' as a kind of superior instance within which the miracle of melting the individual will into the general will takes place." Public opinion is not representative of individual mindsets or interests; it is, in the form of a numerical election result, a "miracle" that produces unity: "What the individuals actually have in mind (*meinen*) (if anything at all) when they mark ballots, remains unknown. This alone is occasion enough not to . . . conceive of public opinion (*Meinung*) as the general expression of the opinions of individuals."[8] What opinions people have, that is, what they "have in mind" or what they "mean" (*meinen*), has not much to do with "public opinion" (*öffentliche Meinung*). People's opinions (in the sense of their thoughts, beliefs, feelings, etc.) are far too diverse and idiosyncratic to be adequately expressed in the form of a ballot. An election result does not indicate the incomprehensibly complex mental or volitional states of millions of people. Rather, it serves as a means by which to establish what is called public opinion (as the successor of the "general will," which already for Rousseau, should not have been mistaken for a mere sum of individual wills). Public opinion is a communicative construct that enables the political system to distribute positions and roles. It is not a human or mental phenomenon, but a communicative one—it is a social construct (one that, given the current electoral procedures, is produced by the "structural coupling" of the political and the mass media system). By the symbolic act of free elections society legitimizes a government to fulfill this function, and, miraculously, in the form of a "mystic transformation," generate a general will of the people.[9]

There is a passage in one of Luhmann's last published articles in which he stresses the symbolic core of democratic politics:

> If one should wish, in accordance with an old convention, to designate this as "rule" of the people, then it seems appropriate to adopt the old distinction between symbolic and instrumental politics.

Given this, what we are dealing with can only be symbolic rule. Symbolic are operations that actualize the unity of the separate and thus have an effect on it—which in this case is the unity of the structural differentiation of the organization of the state, political parties, and the audience. The problem with this distinction is that it is connected with a criticism and a demand to cross the boundaries between the symbolic and the instrumental, that is, the demand for "more democracy" and that the latent function of the political election, namely to secure that the future remains unknown, is overlooked.[10]

This very dense passage is in need of some dissection. First, Luhmann somewhat sarcastically refers to the notion of democracy as a rather obsolete "old convention" that cannot be taken too seriously if it is meant to designate the "rule of the people." If, however, one is inclined to rescue the term, then one would have to admit, according to Luhmann, that it does not designate an actual or instrumental ruling of society, but a symbolic ruling. By alluding to its ancient Greek meaning, a "symbol" can be understood as something that connects or unites what otherwise would be apart. Luhmann mentions the three elements of the political system that he identified in his later works: the state (government, Parliament, administration), the political organizations (the parties), and the audience, that is, the electorate. These are functionally differentiated, and yet coupled; they are distinct, but cooperate within the political system. Because democracy is a form of "rule" (this term has to be used with caution given that, in a strict sense, there is no "ruling" system in our society) that integrates the audience in its constitution of power, its essential feature is that through general elections these three realms of politics are united into a circle: in elections the audience establishes a numerical result that determines the political strength of the various parties which in turn enables the system to form a parliament, a government, and so on. This unity is, according to Luhmann, of a "mythical" nature, since it is based on such narratives as that of a mysterious "will of the people" that somehow expresses itself in politics. However, operating on the basis of a symbolic myth does not prevent democracy from functioning well.

Problems may arise if the mythical aspect of democracy is taken too literally. The demand for an "instrumental democracy" that constitutes more than a "merely" mythical rule of the people may, in fact, pose a danger to democracy because it is an impossible demand. In a sense, the greatest danger for a democracy is to mistake its symbolic nature as real and let the people try to take over, which may result in anarchy, oligarchy, the despotism of a self-styled "people's party," or a meaningless democratic media theatre. Paradoxically, a significant danger for the functioning of democracy is the demand for more democracy.

Such a demand, as Luhmann concludes, implies the urge for a more decisive social impact of democratic procedures, such as elections. But, for Luhmann, the limited social impact of democratic procedures is exactly what makes them so functional. Every election in a functioning democratic system is merely one election before another—just as a season in professional sports always leaves hope for the next one—and does not decide forever the future of a society or a state. If a democratic election is supposed to be an actual instrument for "realizing" the will of the people, this may well be the end of democracy. One of the most important functions of democratic elections is that they do *not* decide a society's fate once and for all.

I conclude this section by addressing two issues that go beyond a descriptive analysis of the radical aspects of Luhmann's theory of democracy. The first issue concerns an implicit conclusion that follows from Luhmann's analysis, namely that politicizing society too intensely may pose a danger for "actually existing democracies." The second is the question of where Luhmann actually stood politically.

In existing democracies there is considerable concern regarding political education. From a liberal perspective, political education is not understood as propaganda or indoctrination, but rather as teaching the young about various political options, about the functioning and meaning of democracy, about how to become an active participant in politics, and how to constructively contribute to the further development of democracy. The dearth of political activity among the citizenry is often lamented (in the mass media). When the "alarmingly" low percentage of voters is published, the media and the politicians seem to worry. There are public campaigns funded by tax money to encourage people to cast their votes. It is often stated that which (democratic) party you vote for does not really matter; what really counts in elections, as in the Olympics, is participation. As the slogan goes in German: *Dabeisein ist alles* (taking part is everything). Historically, concern about political education has had a lot to do with the ideal of democratic citizenship that was a cornerstone of both the American and the French revolutions. Only a politically active member of society is a good member of society, only he (and, somewhat later, she) deserves the honor of living in a truly free and self-managing country. Just as a citizen needs a democracy in order to be a true citizen, a democracy needs politically active citizens in order to be a true democracy. The dependency is mutual.

The reasons why political education (in schools, through the mass media, and through political organizations) is seen as crucial for a functioning democracy are, from a Luhmannian perspective, quite obvious. First, without politically engaged citizens—and just casting your vote on election day already makes one count as politically engaged—the myth of determining the "people's will" loses its magical power. If only a third of the people vote, then something seems to be wrong with the people's willpower. If the most important ceremony for generating the people's will is not well attended, then the people's will is in jeopardy. This is why taxpayers buy television commercials to encourage themselves to vote. There is no mathematical or procedural problem with a low voter turnout (the number of parliamentary seats can be calculated equally well on the basis of ten thousand or ten million votes), but there may be a mythological one. Only a decent turnout at the election guarantees the survival and strength of the democratic myth. The legitimacy of the government, as well as that of the democratic state as a whole, depends on this myth.

A similar ideal was of prime importance for the political self-description of the totalitarian "democracies" in communist and fascist states. The "people's parties" that ruled these states conceived of themselves as both the institutionalized form of public political activity and the source of a thorough politicization of society. The insistence on active political participation followed the very same democratic revolutionary demands stemming from the Enlightenment that still inform liberal democracies—the demand for active citizenship. The despotic democracies of the left and the right saw themselves as more democratic than liberal ones, not less so. And they held an even greater belief in the primacy of political activity. In these states every activity was (potentially) political. Going to school, taking part in sports, or going to one's job, everything was seen as somehow contributing to the strengthening of the people's political progress. Political liberation was a never-ending project. Students, athletes, workers, and teachers, all were constantly taking part in the politicization and political emancipation of the people. The masses were supposed to permanently engage in political self-education. Politically emancipated workers were supposed to conceive of work as political engagement; politically emancipated athletes were supposed to conceive of their efforts in the context of the socialist reconstruction of society (be it leftist or rightist socialism). These societies also measured their political success by the political participation of their citizens. Political mass ceremonies such as big parades and (rigged) elections were considered central for constructing the democratic myth in these despotic states, just as (free) elections are in liberal democracies.

The forced political activism in despotic democracies produced less stability than the merely encouraged political activism in actually existing democracies. Just as the elections were rigged, and *known* to be rigged, so were the mass parades. This proved far more detrimental to the political mythology than mere political indifference has in the West. The belief of the ruling party that political engagement could be steered proved to be wrong. These states, paradoxically, ultimately became victims of an overdose of political education and agitation. The political myth that secures a functioning democracy is rather sensitive to communicative climate change: it can be threatened by too much coldness when it is in danger of being forgotten by the people, but also by too much heat when it is prescribed in the manner of an overdose. A myth remains a myth only when it is neither neglected nor turned into something that is supposed to be more than a myth, namely the truth. True democracy is more than the myth of democracy can stand—it can be the death of democracy. Demands for such a democracy and an intensified politicization of society should therefore be met with caution.

There are two common classifications of Luhmann's political positions, and I find both problematic. The first, and better known, is the accusation that he was a conservative. It is easy to see how this classification came about. In the debate with Habermas in the 1970s, which made him rather famous in Germany, Luhmann was obviously not on the left (as represented by Habermas), so the immediate conclusion by the left was that he was on the right. This is so, because, from the perspective of the left, everything that was not left was an obstacle to social progress and thus necessarily right, or conservative. The various leftist criticisms of Luhmann have been concisely and profoundly listed, analyzed, and refuted by Michael King and Chris Thornhill, and there is nothing I have to add to what they say.[11]

A second, more appropriate, though still somewhat limited, assessment of Luhmann's political position is that he is an advocate of functional differentiation, and that this advocacy also makes him an advocate of "actually existing democracy" given that it enables the perpetuation of functional differentiation and thus contributes to social stability and evolution. Simply put, this amounts to saying that Luhmann not only tries to describe contemporary society, but also that he is happy with the result of his description, that he praises our present society (in the West)— though not necessarily in a Leibnizian fashion as "the best of all possible worlds"— and that he affirms current social structures in the hope that they will be sustained. The function of democratic politics within functional differentiation would accordingly be to remain autopoietic and not to interfere too actively in the functioning of other systems. Such a position would be compatible with, though not exactly equal to, a laissez faire approach to politics— and its relation, in particular, to the economy.

I admit that Luhmann often expressed such an affirmative attitude toward certain aspects of functional differentiation and also suggested that it would probably be better for society to simply continue along these lines rather than trying to introduce "revolutionary" changes. He was particularly concerned with the possibly negative effects of a reduction of functional differentiation. I would argue, however, that these normative slips of an otherwise explicitly antinormative and strictly descriptive theorist should be understood more as occasional pragmatic remarks than as ideological commitments. I think that the conclusion reached by Edwin Czerwick overstates Luhmann's affirmation of democracy: "His [Luhmann's] systems-theoretically inspired conception of democracy has to be seen as an important attempt at (re)constructing the democracies of the Western world from the perspective of the logic or rationality of political systems that today can only appropriately fulfill their social functions if they practice democracy. Democracy thus becomes in effect the most important condition for the continued existence of political systems that have reached a certain evolutionary stage."[12]

Luhmann, on the one hand, was clearly not seeking the abandonment of democracy on the grounds that it is based on a myth or because it would not work well. On the other hand, he did not believe that democracy is the only political structure that would allow for the survival of politics in present society. His defense of democracy is much less specific and, I think, not meant as a plea for democracy. It is meant instead as a warning for those who expect too much from democracy and who want to make society more democratic. He was, I believe, quite disturbed by ideological attempts at taking democracy too seriously and thought that such attempts may paradoxically pose a danger for its existence. I think that Luhmann was no prescriptive thinker, and perhaps even more importantly, a highly non- or even anti-ideological thinker. He looked at the totalitarian political systems that were established on the foundations of leftist or rightist ideologies with great dismay. He was also very sensitive about the problems of "ideologizing" liberal democracy. To criticize current liberal democracy and to demand that it should be "really" democratic smacks of democratic "fundamentalism" and thus of ideological fervor. I think that Luhmann's affirmation of democracy and of functional differentiation only says that functional differentiation is a bearable outcome of social evolution and that attempts to interfere in evolutionary processes to help it progress are usually not very promising. His defense of democracy is thus not an expression of a substantial prodemocratic ideology. It is based, instead, on the paradoxical insight that politically less charged political systems seem to function in a way that is socially less harmful than those of a highly ideological nature. The benefit of actually existing democracy is not that it somehow realizes any supposed historical goal, but that it allows for social stability. Luhmann believed that "symbolic democracy" had empirically proven to be more successful than any attempt to bring about "true democracy."

NINE

CONCLUSION
NEC SPE NEC METU: NEITHER HOPE NOR FEAR

A German friend of mine, although generally sympathetic to social systems theory, once expressed a certain frustration that, as he said, not only he himself but many others had experienced when studying Luhmann. Creating a very fitting metaphor, he pointed out that Luhmann's works do not provide its readers with a Kuschelecke, literally, a "cuddling corner," a space with well-cushioned furniture that allows readers to feel comforted and cozy, relaxed and warm.[1] Since he made that remark, I have been on the search for Luhmann's cuddling corner, so far to no avail. Perhaps it is this complete lack that makes Luhmann so radical—or is it?

Attempts to make Luhmann a little cozier and more comforting are not uncommon among his interpreters.[2] Apparently, for them the longing for a *Kuschelecke* became irresistible. Such efforts to soften Luhmann are, I think, generally unhelpful. To my mind, a watered-down Luhmann, a Luhmann whose radicalism is ignored or tempered, only leads to misunderstandings and distortions. This is not what his "supertheory" deserves. It is, in my view, better to harshly criticize Luhmann for his radicalism than to apologetically deny it. To salvage, preserve, and clarify Luhmann's radicalism has been my main purpose in writing this book.

So far, I have attempted to explain Luhmann's radical departure from mainstream social theory and modern Western philosophy by pointing out several specific areas in which Luhmann's theory represents a paradigm shift. These areas range from his anti- or posthumanism to his deconstruction of democracy. I conclude with a more general account of Luhmann's radicalism. The questions I address in these final remarks are Where does Luhmann's radicalism lead? In what ways does one see the world differently after understanding Luhmann? What would a Luhmannian attitude toward society, the world, and, indeed, one's life consist of? Such questions were hardly an issue for Luhmann himself, given that they go beyond the scope of the theory and may therefore even be considered indecent or inappropriate to ask. Nevertheless, I could not refrain from asking them, if only to look for and establish, if not a *Kuschelecke*, than at least something to make up for its lack.

The major paradigm shift that I ascribe to Luhmann consists in the end of philosophy and the beginning of theory.[3] Such a change has theoretical consequences: in the same way as the shift from religion to philosophy in early modern Europe, from the sacred to the secular, came alongside shifts of social semantics and social structures, the shift from philosophy to theory will be accompanied by what may be called, for lack of a better phrase, shifts in attitude. A disenchantment with or a liberation from the sacred and divine world of theology may be followed by a disenchantment with or liberation from the rational and moral world of philosophy. It would be foolish to try to predict what a postphilosophical semantics would look like, but it may be possible to outline some of the features of an attitude that emerges from observing Luhmann as one of the first postphilosophical theorists. Three closely interconnected features of this attitude seem to be modesty,[4] irony, and equanimity. These constitute, so to speak, the core of the virtue ethics of social systems theory.[5]

Modesty

The period of the European Renaissance and the Enlightenment brought about the reemergence and re-creation of "greater science"— in the sense of the German term *Wissenschaft*: an organized and institutionalized effort, including all academic disciplines, that is, natural and social sciences and the humanities alike, for the sake of producing knowledge and making it available to society. In early modernity, philosophy was still perceived as—and thought of itself as—being at the helm of this endeavor.[6] This was certainly true for Kant and Hegel and was not essentially different for Marx or Darwin. Modern philosophy, up to and including at least the nineteenth century, was epistemologically optimistic. It was generally believed that "greater science" would discover all sorts of truth and thereby enlighten and empower humankind. It was to be the driving force behind social, technological, and ethical improvements. Historically speaking, philosophy has been at the center of the modern ambition to produce knowledge and, thereby, to progress.

In the twentieth century, philosophy was increasingly pushed to the margins of what was considered scientific activity. Notwithstanding this decline, and the increasing detachment of philosophy from science, it is still rather common to identify our times with terms such as "information age" or "knowledge society." In this way, the semantics of Enlightenment philosophy lives on. To have knowledge and to possess information is seen as the key to social success and to personal development. In order to be a democratic citizen, an autonomous human being, a free individual, one needs to know things and to have access to information. Education is generally believed to be the most important foundation for building a thriving society and for becoming an independent individual. The German term *Bildung,* which plays a central role in Hegel's philosophy, expresses this nicely: it means both education and edification, both the imparting and acquisition of knowledge and the "building" (the German term's etymological counterpart in English) of a person's character or a nation's culture. *Bildung,* once identified with philosophy, has become a general project and ambition of any modern society. In this way, we still live in a "philosophical" society. Modern society conceives of itself as being permanently engaged in its own *Bildung* through the production of knowledge and the continual quest for self-improvement and the discovery of truths.

From the perspective of theory, however, the epistemological optimism involved in a "knowledge society" is questionable. Theory describes the production of knowledge as a form of communication, of social construction. It does not, to be sure, replace the philosophical epistemological optimism with a simple pessimism, denouncing the usefulness of knowledge altogether. However, from the perspective of theory, the soteriological hopes that are connected with the increase in the production of knowledge seem unwarranted. As a social construct, knowledge enables society and individuals to do a lot of things that they would otherwise have been unable to do—I could not, for instance, write and publish this book if society were not interested in knowledge production—but this does not mean that society or individuals actually get closer to truth. In a functionally differentiated society, science cannot do what philosophy was once assumed to do, namely to initiate an encompassing process of *Bildung* in the sense outlined above.

The traditional philosophical approach toward the production of knowledge assumed that there was both a collective subject and an individual one to be improved. From the perspective of theory, no such subjects exist. No one "has" knowledge as an internal component of himself (or herself). Knowledge functions, like money and like power, as a generalized medium of communication. And one "has" it in the ways one has other media (in systems-theoretical terms) that are attributed a certain value in a particular social context. Knowledge allows society to function, but does not essentially improve an individual or a society as a whole. From the perspective of theory, more knowledge does not lead to more *Bildung* anymore than more money or more power does.

The inflation of knowledge seems an excellent example of this. No person—and no nation or country or social system—is able to coherently accumulate or store knowledge. In fact, knowledge only counts if it is *exchanged* and thus given away or spent. It is exchanged communicatively (in academic publications, for instance) as well as temporally: new knowledge replaces old knowledge.[7] The idea of "absolute knowledge" (to use Hegel's term) is no longer tenable from the perspective of theory. If knowledge is a medium, like money or power, then those who take part in its production have no reason to believe they are taking part in an ultimately self-improving endeavor. In other words, theorists have to be more modest than the philosophers of old. They can no longer proudly consider themselves all-important lovers of wisdom. Instead, they must consider themselves traders at the knowledge exchange marketplace. Theorists will have to let go of a lot of the pretension that used to be attached to the profession of philosophy.

When Marx claimed to have flipped Hegel from his head to his feet, he meant not only that he had converted Hegel's idealism into materialism, but also that he finally made "philosophical science" (Hegel's *philosophische Wissenschaft*) practically applicable rather than merely spiritually enlightening. Marx stated this succinctly in thesis eleven on Feuerbach: "Philosophers have hitherto only interpreted the world in various ways; the point is to change it."[8] The idea of changing the world through philosophical science, however, is no less Hegelian than Marxist. Philosophical interpretations, for Hegel and his predecessors, were always supposed to change the world. It was the very project of a "philosophical science," or, in Kantian terms, of a "future metaphysics that will be able to present itself as science." Once philosophy succeeds in overcoming the "scandal of philosophy" and transforms itself into science, it cannot fail to change the world. Hegel often uses the expression *wirkliches Wissen,* which means "true knowledge" (as opposed to apparent and thus false knowledge) and denotes "effective knowledge" (*wirken* means "to be effective"). If scientific philosophy is true, it cannot but have an immediate effect on the world. In this way, Enlightenment philosophy was not only about the production of knowledge, but, right from the start (and not only with Marx) also about changing the world.

Philosophy not only implied that knowing the world was possible, but also that intervening in society and foreseeing and directing its change and development was a possibility. For Kant, philosophy would eventually show the way to "eternal peace." For Marx, philosophy would help to bring about the end of class antagonisms. The figure of the philosopher has thus been regularly identified with a visionary, a secular alternative to the religious messiah. The visionary attitude of philosophers can, as with Kant and Marx, be found on the level of "grand theory," but it can also be detected on a much smaller scale in the pronouncements of countless normative philosophers of our day. Political philosophers and applied ethicists typically feel competent to present suggestions for social or moral change.

Theory disconnects itself from the interventionist heritage of philosophical science. Theory admits, however, that it does change the world. The world—and, in particular, society—is slightly different once this very book is published, for instance. Whatever happens within society contributes to its evolution, just as whatever happens within an ecosystem has an effect on its further development. The difference between interventionist philosophy and noninterventionist theory is not that the latter would deny that philosophizing and theorizing make a difference, but how they evaluate and analyze their making of differences.

Luhmann's theory is neither idealist nor materialist; it is constructivist. Like idealists who claim that different ideas change society and materialists who claim that material changes change society, constructivists claim that different social constructions constitute social change. This is not the issue. The issue is that ideas and material conditions are supposed to be something more essential than a social construct—in other words, whereas ideas or material conditions are supposed to be foundational first causes of social change, social constructs are radically immanent within society and no more a cause of social change than its effect. Theory is, at the same time, both about society and within society. A theory of society (in the grammatically ambiguous sense of *genitivus objectivus* and *genitivus subjectivus*) is a product of the very society it theorizes about.[9] Theory cannot initiate a specific change toward a certain goal; it simply plays a (relatively minor) part in the continual self-modification of society.

Social theory, in the strict sense of the word "theory," unlike political philosophy, cannot conceive of a difference between "merely" interpreting the world and changing it. For Marx (as well as many non-Marxist political philosophers) political theory should not simply provide another idle interpretation of society, but do something essentially different, namely introduce material change. For theory, however, society consists of nothing but communication. Theory, therefore, cannot directly change the world, it can only change society, and in a hypercomplex world, it is never predictable in what ways social changes will change the world. While, on the one hand, it is unavoidable that theory changes society and the world, on the other hand, there is no mechanical causal link between changes in theory and changes in the world. Thus, in a strict sense, any normative theoretical intervention in the world is impossible. Theorists change the world, but they cannot claim to be in a position to control, predict, or even speak truthfully about these changes. Such is what constitutes Luhmann's radical theoretical modesty.

Irony

By being engaged in the production of knowledge and its exchange, theory produces and trades meaning, or sense (which is perhaps the better translation for the German term *Sinn* used by Luhmann). To be sure, all communication constructs sense in the systems-theoretical meaning of this term. Sense is the most general medium of society as conceived by Luhmann, and, moreover, is essential for making the structural coupling between psychic systems and communication systems—between human minds and society—possible. Sense is constructed when we think and when we communicate. Specific social systems operate by constructing specifically meaningful media (such as money in the economy). In this way, what the economy is all about, is making money. In the same way, the science system (in which theory and philosophy are housed) is all about making truth. The meaning of these systems is their specific construction of social sense. They provide society with unique sources of sense. Other systems do the same. Religion, for instance, contributes religious sense to society; the legal system makes the distinction between legality and illegality meaningful; and the health system makes health a sensible social concern.

The very plurality and incommensurability of sense in society, however, makes sense, in a certain way, meaningless and makes it run counter to what is perhaps the most simplified traditional definition of philosophy. In Plato's *Apology*, Socrates famously declares that the unexamined life is not worth living.[10] This pronouncement could serve as the locus classicus for understanding philosophy as a systematic effort to discover the meaning, or, as I should say here, the "sense of life" (*Sinn des Lebens*). In this traditional philosophical context, sense is grammatically singular. Strictly speaking, for philosophy—particularly in the German-speaking context to which Luhmann reacted—sense could not be diversified without being in danger of becoming nonsense. In the plural, the German word *der Sinn* turns into *die Sinne,* which does not mean "meanings," but "the senses." From a Platonic perspective, this signifies that a pluralized sense loses its intellectual and rational meaning and degenerates into something physical and irrational. The pluralizing of sense thus amounts to its bastardization and a paradoxical reversal into its opposite.

In his later writings, Luhmann typically avoided referencing Husserl when using the term *Sinn,* turning instead to Deleuze's *Logique du sens.*[11] The "logic of sense," in theory, is, so to speak, a perversion of the philosophically inherited logic of sense. Instead of being devoted to *die Logik* (in the singular) and *der Sinn* (in the singular), theory explores the various possibilities of multiple and simultaneous logical and sense constructions. The radical pluralizing of sense not only marks a conspicuous departure from the quintessential philosophical attempt to discover the meaning of life, but also a shift in style or attitude. Socrates, although from time to time operating with Socratic irony, was dead serious about the examination of life, as is well illustrated in the *Apology.* Compared with Socratic irony, theory, when shifting to a plurality of sense, introduces a far more radical way of being ironic. Luhmann states: "Self-critical reason is ironical reason. It is the reason of 'the gypsies who constantly vagabond around Europe.'"[12] In direct opposition to his earlier master Husserl, toward the end of his life Luhmann identified himself with the gypsies of reason—those who violate the unified pattern of sense-making and live outside of what is generally considered the norm. Luhmann's shift from Husserl's *Sinn* to Deleuze's *sens* can be understood as an indicator of what I am calling the shift from philosophy to theory. It goes along with making reason ironical.

In my personal definition, irony is not simply saying (or communicating) something that is supposed to be understood as the opposite of what is actually being said (such as to say "great!" when something that is obviously not great is happening), but rather saying something that is at the same time, and to the same extent, both serious and not serious, both valid and invalid. It makes sense, but at the same time and to the same extent it also "makes nonsense." An example of this is the sentence at the end of Luhmann's preface to *The Science of Society*: "It remains only to say, as usual, that any remaining errors are chargeable to me—with the exception of errors in this sentence, obviously!"[13] Luhmann, obviously, does not indicate, to the contrary of what is being said, that the responsibility for errors in his book rests with those whom he has just thanked for their help and assistance. Instead, he fully assumes the responsibility for the remaining errors in his book, but, at the same time, and to the same extent, he points out the stereotypical and, from a theoretical perspective, meaningless character of such a rhetorical gesture. The sentence constructs sense (assuming the responsibility for errors) and nonsense (pointing out the meaninglessness of such an assumption of responsibility) at the same time and to the same extent. The sentence is therefore not only perfomatively ironical, but also expresses the ironical aspect of Luhmann's theory: if the scientific construction of knowledge (which is the very topic of the scientific book that this sentence is included in) is a contingent construction of (in the traditional philosophical sense) ultimately meaningless sense, then to point this out in the context of a scientific theoretical treatise is ultimately meaningless as well. At the same time, however, the fact of communicating this makes a lot of sense, which is the very point of theory. Ironically, this point becomes its ultimate meaning.

Luhmann's theory is about the contingent social constructions of sense that have no ultimate meaning, no transcendental or transcendent anchorage, and do not manifest or conform to a unified reason. In this way, theoretical reason is ironical reason: what it says is rooted in contingency and not necessity, and this is also the case "autologically." Self-critical reason takes into account that it is ironical, and one of the ways to take this into account is to use ironical communication. Ironical reason is not only "logically" ironical, it is also ironical in style. In this way, for Luhmann, irony is not simply a didactical or dialectical method, as it was for Socrates or Plato; it is an integral aspect of the "autological" character of theory. In traditional philosophy, irony was a tool and could be applied or not. Theory is an exercise in ironical reason; it is, so to speak, a performance by the gypsies of reason.

A centerpiece of all of the philosophical sciences has always been moral science, or ethics. If theory ironically undermines philosophical meaning, then it cannot fail to ironically deconstruct this field that has usually been taken as most serious by those engaged in it. The ironical attitude toward ethics is therefore potentially the most controversial, provocative, and radical aspect of Luhmann's theory.

Luhmann's redefinition of ethics is another example of his irony.[14] He first defines morality as the communicative distinction between, and distribution of, esteem and disesteem. He goes on to define ethics as the "reflective theory of morality" (*Reflexionstheorie der Moral*). Whereas philosophical ethics, according to Luhmann, tried to identify to what extent reason was inherent in morality, Luhmann's reflective theory takes a different approach: It shows that traditional attempts to identify moral reason have failed, and that the function of theoretical ethics, as opposed to philosophical ethics, can only be to warn of morality. The shift from philosophical ethics to theoretical ethics is a shift from serious ethics to ironical ethics. Ethics is no longer the scientific (in the sense of philosophical science) search for moral reason, but the "deconstruction" of moral communication.[15] Ethical theory shows the sense and nonsense of morality at the same time. Philosophical ethics had focused on its sense alone.

An ironical ethics is also self-critical. This does not mean, in a traditional moral sense, that an ethicist should critically examine his or her own moral behavior, but that ethics must include a reflection on the limitations and contingency of its meaning. Philosophical ethics, simply speaking, attempts to identify the correct application or meaning of the moral distinction between good and bad, or, more precisely, between good and evil. Theoretical ethics, on the other hand, outlines how this very attempt is, to use Nietzsche's phrase, "beyond good and evil." Ethical philosophy cannot but assume that it is good and advocate the goodness it establishes. Ethical theory, on the other hand, looks at morality as one form of contingent sense construction. The theoretical reflection on this sense construction is itself just as contingent as morality. From this perspective, neither morality nor its theory is good or bad. Ethical theory does not and cannot tell society what is ultimately good or bad, only what sort of nonsense is implied in ethical sense-making.

In the case of Luhmann's ethics, he points out the dangers of moral communication and its social pathologies. Ironical reason, when applied to ethics, results in "negative ethics." Luhmann's proclamation that ethics is supposed to warn of morality thus has to be understood ironically: if taken too seriously, if taken as the ethical claim that morality is ultimately bad or evil, it would have to warn of itself and no longer be self-critical. In this way, perhaps the most important aspect of the shift from philosophical ethics to theoretical ethics lies in a shift from advocating a serious morality to an exercise in (self-)ironical reason. A major problem with traditional philosophical ethics is that it lacks the capacity to seriously consider its own nonsense. In this way, not only science, but even ethics, can now become, at least in theory, "gay" (in the Nietzschean sense of *fröhlich*).

Equanimity

Nonironical ethics, particularly in social and political contexts, tends to apply rhetorical "shock and awe" strategies. In Luhmann's immediate social environment, that is, post–World War II Germany from the 1960s to the 1990s, the new left, both in academia and in politics, used such communicative tools. First, moral outrage was created—about the Nazi background of the parent generation; about the Vietnam war and American imperialism; about the capitalist *Schweinesystem* (pig system); about the nuclear arms race; about unfair trade mechanisms; about human rights violations; about nuclear power plants, the dying of the forests, and other environmental disasters, and so on. Then, beautiful countervisions were suggested: political and sexual liberation, an economy based on fairness and nonprofit orientation, political justice and equal rights for all, pacifism and disarmament, wind and solar power, a green conscience, and so on. The most prominent of Luhmann's opponents on the German left, Jürgen Habermas, the proponent of a "discourse without domination" (*herrschatsfreier Diskurs*), and Ulrich Beck with his reflections on "risk society" (*Risikogesellschaft*), are good examples of these techniques. Moral communication, as Luhmann pointed out in his writings on ethics, functions by highlighting the scandalous and by contrasting it, at least implicitly, with a cathartically relieving remedy. In this way, nonironical ethics and nonironical reason produce a lot of social and psychological heat: they are exciting. People will be shocked, be enraged, and feel threatened by being alerted to all the bad and catastrophic things around them that they hadn't really been aware of, as well as awed, enamored, and passionate about the wonderful solutions that are just around the corner if society would only complete its own enlightenment. Nonironic shock and awe morality, in other words, operates by fuelling both fears and hopes. It depicts images of hell, but also offers a *Kuschelecke* for relaxation.

The Luhmannian attitude to society, with all its pain and joy, with its perils and consolations, is strikingly different. Of course, Luhmann's theory is not blind to the suffering that "exists on a massive scale and in such forms that are beyond description" in today's world.[16] Rather than following the impulse to react to these circumstances with shock and awe, however, theory takes on an alternative stance: *nec spe nec metu* (neither hope nor fear), an ancient Latin phrase that Luhmann somewhat playfully uses to advocate "a kind of stoic attitude" in social theory,[17] and thus, if such an extension may be allowed, toward the world in general.

In my view, this phrase can serve as an answer to the perhaps inappropriate question posed at the beginning of this chapter: where is one led by Luhmann's radicalism? It leads one, I believe, to an attitude that combines practical (but not ontological or epistemological) aspects of several historically and geographically different, but nevertheless similar, philosophies: Stoicism, Spinozism, and Daoism. Paradoxically, or ironically, Luhmann's radical postphilosophical theory thus connects back, in its existential dimension, with some of the most traditional teachings of wisdom in the history of philosophy.

Luhmann's theory, as I have outlined it, confronts humankind with the "sociological insult," the insight into the limits of social steering. We are not at the center of the cosmos, we are not the "crown of creation," and we are not the masters of our own minds; nor are we the autonomous creators of the social world. Previous attempts to use philosophical insights and wisdom to improve society have failed spectacularly. Theory recognizes not our total impotence but the relative helplessness of philosophical and ideological interventionism. Theory does not equal a fatalistic pessimism, but a Stoic acceptance of the basic "human condition" of exposure to an uncontrollable environment. Rather than reacting to this insult with indignation and rage, with a Promethean activism, an attempt to overpower the gods, so to speak, theory opts instead for calmness and deference. This attitude is not to be mistaken for a sheepish obedience or submission. It consists in the insight of (self-)ironic reason that its power consists in making sense of and in the world rather than in deliberately changing the world into something altogether different.

The Stoic aspect of theory allows the theoretician to develop a potential for tolerating the otherwise nearly intolerable. The insight of theory into its inability to take control in the world and steer society towards a land of milk and honey does not lead to mental paralysis or defeatism, but to relaxation and alleviation. Dramatically put, one can say that nonironic reason hardens whereas ironical reason lightens. It is not tragic that political decisions cannot essentially decide anything about the future of society or mankind; it is rather a form of pressure release. That no ultimately decisive decisions are possible makes coming to a decision less difficult, not more so. "Stoic politics" will hardly become fundamentalist; there is not enough at stake. Room for contingency leaves, metaphorically speaking, some breathing room. Or, ironically speaking, theory helps us to see—and *do*—things more philosophically.

It is not that we cannot do anything, nor is there any need to believe that all depends on us getting it right. Stoic theory does not discourage people from engaging in politics or social work, or, for that matter, from doing anything whatsoever, it merely aims at discouraging us from adopting the activist—and sometimes philosophical—vanity that the fate of the world rests primarily with us. Politically speaking, the Stoic aspect of theory may be equated with its anti-ideological stance. It distrusts utopian programs and agendas, and because that is so, it can ally itself rather easily with realist and pragmatic approaches to politics that try to avoid the traps of either overenthusiastic hopes or numbing fears.

A Spinozist element of theory can be found in its acknowledgment of various levels of knowledge. Theoretical knowledge may be described as an ironical transformation of Spinoza's third kind of knowledge, that is, knowledge *sub specie aeternitatis*. Theoretical knowledge is different from other kinds of knowledge, namely common everyday knowledge (such as the knowledge of the way to drive to town) and nontheoretical reflective knowledge (knowledge in the natural sciences, for instance). The various kinds of knowledge are neither congruent nor incompatible with one another. To excel in one kind of knowledge is not indicative of how well one does in another. A theorist may not be good at driving or at repairing cars; a mechanic might not understand theory. This brings certain blessings. On the one hand, it makes theoretical knowledge, unlike religious or traditional philosophical knowledge, contingent. It is not necessary for anyone to have it. One can live well without it, and the world is not lost altogether if it is not being revealed. On the other hand, theorists cannot expect, unlike saints or philosophical sages, that their theoretical excellence will make them a more accomplished person than anyone else. Theoretical knowledge is innocent; it does not come with a mission, with the implicit duty to impart it to all others, or with the implication that it will change its possessor into a flawless being. In this way, it absolves those who have it from unreasonable demands, and it spares those who lack it from attempts to convert them.

Theoretical expertise is a rare characteristic among people; it is rather esoteric. It is difficult to achieve and does not necessarily bring great social prestige. At best, one may get a relatively well-paid job that leaves one with a lot of time to further engage in theory. However, it can provide its possessors with a number of mental benefits. One will be able to understand or interpret—in theoretical language, to observe—the world from a unique perspective of excluded inclusion. One will see that one's point of observation, while certainly within the world and not beyond it in any way, is nevertheless inaccessible to those who do not do theory. To be able to look at the world, including oneself, *sub specie theoriae* therefore comes with some psychological benefits. It is not only an exercise in communication, but also likely to be accompanied by unique mental operations that can be experienced as extraordinarily clear and distinct. Such a theoretical state of mind may well be gratifying for the possessor since it does not give rise to anxiety or euphoria. It is also quite different from what Wittgenstein once described as the experience "of feeling absolutely safe" or "safe in the hands of God."[18]

Given the nonecstatic equanimity that theorists may enjoy and display in their theoretical communication, they are well positioned to enrich society with the same. Theory operates with a radical *Gelassenheit,* or intellectual and communicational ease. This may be called its Daoist aspect. Thus, if Luhmann is not able to come up with a *Kuschelecke,* he at least offers a sort of yoga mat.

Niklas Luhmann was born on December 8, 1927, in Lüneburg, Germany, a small city to the southeast of Hamburg. His father owned a brewery and was a member of the local business community. Luhmann spent his childhood in the "Nazi environment."[1] As was practically mandatory at the time, he became a member of the Hitler-Jugend, the fascist youth organization, at an early age. He recalled this experience as rather unpleasant because of all the marching and greeting he had to do. At the age of fifteen, he underwent military training as an air force assistant. At the end of 1944, he was conscripted as a soldier at the front and was soon captured by American forces. He was released shortly after his capture because he was not yet eighteen years of age.

After the Second World War, Luhmann studied law. This decision was influenced by the violations of the Geneva Convention he had witnessed during his time as a POW (he had been beaten, and some of his fellow POWs who were older than eighteen had been sent to work in French mines). He studied at the University in Freiburg, focusing on the history of Roman law, and obtained his first degree in 1949, followed by an internship with a lawyer in his hometown. Unsatisfied with this line of work, he accepted a position within the legal branch of the regional administration and worked as an assistant to various courts. In the 1950s, he worked for the state administration in the area of regulating claims by Germans who had been mistreated during Nazi times. Luhmann never became a member of any political party. According to Luhmann, his lack of party affiliation was detrimental in pursuing a career as a civil servant, in addition to his disinclination to get drunk at the local firefighter fests.[2] He also felt that his intellectual interests in Descartes, Husserl, the phenomenologist Alfred Schütz, the poet Hölderlin, and other authors did not enhance his prospects of promotion within the administration. He married in 1960; he and his wife, Ursula (d. 1977), had three children.

Having successfully applied for a scholarship he had found advertised in one of the documents processed through his office, Luhmann took a one-year leave from administrative duties in order to study sociology at Harvard University from 1960 to 1961.At Harvard, he became a student of Talcott Parsons and was introduced to social systems theory. In 1962, shortly after his return to Germany, he took on a position within a research institution at the academy for administration in Speyer. In 1966, Luhmann obtained first his Ph.D., then his *Habilitation* (a second advanced degree that was necessary to be eligible for a university professorship in Germany), and was offered a position at the University of Bielefeld, which had been newly established under the academic direction of Helmut Schelsky, a leading German sociologist and intellectual of the time. Between 1963 and 1966 Luhmann authored or coauthored seven books and various articles on administrative and sociological topics.[3]

During his early years as a university teacher, the student protest movement erupted in Germany as well as many other countries. Luhmann found himself "neither on the side of the accused nor of the accusers."[4] When he became a full professor on the faculty of sociology at the University of Bielefeld in 1969, he had to list the research projects he was about to pursue. Luhmann stated that his project was a "theory of society," that the estimated duration was thirty years, and that the costs were zero.[5] He was unsatisfied with the theoretical level of the political and sociological debates of the time and found that none of the classical social thinkers, from Marx to Weber to Durkheim to Simmel, provided an adequate description of contemporary society. He aspired to replace their theories with what he later called a new social "supertheory."[6]

In the early 1970s, Luhmann became famous in the academic world in Germany through the debates he had with the Frankfurt School and, in particular, with its main representative at this time, Jürgen

Habermas. The so-called Habermas-Luhmann or Frankfurt-Bielefeld controversy is best documented in a jointly published volume from 1971: *Theorie der Gesellschaft oder Sozialtechnolgie* (Theory of Society or Social Technology).[7] Habermas's and Luhmann's approaches to an understanding of society were very different from each other. Methodologically speaking, Habermas advocated a critical theory that would contribute to a normative restructuring of society; he expected this theory to help make society more equal, just, fair, and so on. Luhmann opted for a strictly disengaged and descriptive methodology devoid of any ideological inclinations. For Habermas, society constitutes a human "life-world" within which communicative action is supposed to be geared toward mutual understanding. Communication is therefore the most basic social activity of humans, which, if only performed rationally enough, can lead to social consensus and the minimization of domination of some over others. For Luhmann, communication is not based on human interaction. It is the mode by which society operates. According to him, communication systems communicate, not individuals. The economy, for instance, is a communication system that operates through various forms of financial transactions. These transactions constitute the functioning of the economic system, not the human beings who are attributed with, for instance, the ownership of bank accounts. Given the foundational differences between Habermas's normative-humanist approach and Luhmann's descriptive-functional approach, the debate was less a dialogue and more an exchange of irreconcilable positions on what society is and what social theory means. Luhmann stated later in his life that, intellectually speaking, he had not profited very much from the controversy.[8] In Luhmann's view, the debate had been rather fruitless because of the radical differences between his own theoretical stance and Habermas's political agenda.

With the intention of constructing a new social theory that, unlike the theories of the classical authors mentioned above or of the Frankfurt School, would focus primarily on functional aspects of society, Luhmann turned toward the cybernetic and constructivist models that had emerged in the 1950s and 1960s. He used them to develop and modify Parsons's systemic analysis of society. Influenced by authors such as Gregory Bateson, Ernst von Glasersfeld, Heinz von Foerster, and the logician and mathematician George Spencer Brown, he attempted to adopt the shift from a first-order cybernetics that viewed systems as "trivial machines" to a second-order cybernetics of complex machines for *social* systems theory.[9] Luhmann imported cybernetic conceptions of distinction-making, self- and other-reference, and cognitive blind spots into social theory and thereby departed more and more from Parsons. In the 1970s and 1980s Luhmann became interested in the work of the Chilean constructivist evolutionary biologists Humberto Maturana and Francisco Varela and subsequently cooperated with them. In addition to the cybernetic vocabulary, Luhmann integrated their biological concept of *autopoiesis*, their views on system-environmental coevolution, and their ideas about constructive observation, and integrated these into his theory of society and communication.

In 1984, Luhmann's first magnum opus *Soziale Systeme* (translated into English as *Social Systems*) was published. This voluminous book contained a first summary of Luhmann's social "supertheory." In comparison with all of his—already very numerous—earlier publications, he called this book his first "real publication," whereas the previous would merely constitute a "zero-series of theory production."[10] It may therefore be said that Luhmann's social systems theory reached its mature form only with and after the publication of *Social Systems* and the inclusion of the constructivism of second-order cybernetics and evolutionary biology. Given the considerable influence of the latter, Habermas, in a comprehensive analysis of Luhmann's theory, labeled it quite appropriately "metabiological."[11] Just as Greek metaphysics explained the world beyond the physical by applying physical concepts, Luhmann applied biological concepts for a descriptive analysis of the nonbiological world and, in particular, society and communication.

In the decade after the publication of *Social Systems*, which presented an outline of his theory of society as a whole, Luhmann published several volumes concretely depicting the functioning of various subsystems in society, including: *Die Wirtschaft der Gesellschaft* (The Economy of Society, 1988), *Die Wissenschaft der Gesellschaft* (The Science of Society, 1990), *Das Recht der Gesellschaft* (1993, translated into English as *Law as a Social System*), *Die Kunst der Gesellschaft* (1995, translated into English as *Art as a Social System*), and *Die Realität der Massenmedien* (1996, translated into English as *The Reality of the Mass Media*).[12] Volumes on the systems of politics, religion, and education were published posthumously.[13] In 1997, Luhmann presented a new and even more extended summary of his general theory of society in the 1,164-page *Die Gesellschaft der Gesellschaft* (The Society of Society).[14]

In addition to the two general outlines of a theory of society and the concrete descriptions of specific social function systems, Luhmann published a number of works on "social structure and semantics," that is, historical accounts of how structural change in society, or, in other words, the evolution of society, went along with a semantic evolution, namely the development of concepts, values, and vocabularies. Mostly in the form of (often lengthy) articles, Luhmann discussed topics such as the development of the semantics of individuality, morality, and, in the form of the monograph *Liebe als Passion* (1982, translated into English as *Love as Passion*), love.[15]

A fourth kind of publications consists of writings on issues that were of current political relevance. The book *Ökologische Kommunikation* (1986, translated into English as *Ecological Communication*)[16] is a reflection on the communicative success of ecological themes in society and politics (as manifested in the rise to power of the Green Party in Germany). The book *Soziologie des Risikos* (1991, translated into English as *Risk: A Sociological Theory*)[17] can be seen as a reaction to the increasing popularity of the concept of "risk society" suggested by Ulrich Beck. It may well be said that with these two monographs (as well as with a number of related articles) Luhmann continued his earlier debates with the political left. Leftist popular and academic engagement had shifted from the concerns of the Frankfurt School to environmental issues, and Luhmann attempted to "deconstruct" these ideological discourses on the basis of his functionalist understanding of communication.

In the last decade of his life, Luhmann's writings showed an ever increasing awareness and recognition of (French) postmodernism. For instance, Luhmann frequently referred to Deleuze when mentioning his central concept of *Sinn* (sense), which he had initially taken from Husserl. Authors such as Derrida and Lyotard are also continually commented on in Luhmann's later publications. In 1993 Luhmann published the programmatic article "Deconstruction as Second-Order Observing," in which he explicitly affirmed similarities between his approach and the deconstructivist approach.[18] While he always maintained that the term "postmodernity" was misleading—because he believed that the period of modernity had not yet historically come to an end—Luhmann nevertheless declared with regard to his own theory: "is this, after all, a postmodern theory? Maybe, but then the adherents of postmodern conceptions will finally know what they are talking about."[19]

With the publication of *Social Systems,* Luhmann established himself as the most influential German sociologist of his time and one of the major German theoreticians of the second half of the twentieth century. His enormous body of work, about seventy books and close to five hundred articles, was widely used in many disciplines in the social sciences and the humanities. Translations appeared in Italian, Spanish, English, Chinese, Japanese, and other languages, so that the theory became globally accessible (or at least available). Luhmann was awarded the prestigious Hegel Prize in Stuttgart in 1988. In 1993, he became Professor Emeritus, still at the University of Bielefeld. After an increasingly severe illness, he died on November 6, 1998, in his home in Oerlinghausen near the city of Bielefeld. He had completed the thirty-year project that he outlined in 1969 just in time.

Theory of Society

Luhmann's theory of society is, by definition, a theory of communication, since he conceives of society as consisting of communication.[20] For him, "society" means all the communication that is going on. More precisely, he conceives of society as a complex amalgamation of communication *systems.* Therefore, in order to understand Luhmann's theory of communication, one first has to understand the overarching framework of general systems theory, and within this, the narrower framework of *social* systems theory. Luhmann's theory of communication is embedded in this larger theoretical context.

There are two generations of systems theory, and Luhmann is among the representatives of the second one. Conceptions of the latter have been variously described as constituting "second-order systems theory," "second-order cybernetics," or theories of "second-order emergence."[21] In the introduction to *Social Systems*, Luhmann discusses what he calls the "paradigm change in systems theory" by pointing out the switch from a systemic concept based on the distinction whole/parts to one based on the distinction system/environment. One could therefore call second-order systems theory "systems-environment theory" or even "ecological systems theory," though none of these terms have been widely used. Luhmann summarizes the features of second-order systems theory in comparison with its first-order predecessor:

> System differentiation is nothing more than the repetition within systems of the difference between system and environment. Through it, the whole system uses itself as environment in forming its own subsystems and thereby achieves greater improbability on the level of those subsystems by more rigorously filtering an ultimately uncontrollable environment. Accordingly, a differentiated system is no longer simply composed of a relatively large number of parts and the relations among them; rather, it is composed of a large number of operationally employable system/environment differences, which each, along different cutting lines, reconstruct the whole system as the unity of subsystem and environment.[22]

This is typical of Luhmann's dense and highly technical writing. I will try to briefly "decomplexify" it by means of a concrete analogy. This analogy is taken from biology, a science Luhmann himself borrowed heavily from (through Maturana and Varela). A "trivial" concept of the body may view it as a systemic or organic whole of individual parts. These may be, for instance, the organs: the lungs, the heart, the liver, and so on. The body could thus be viewed as a collection of parts that contribute to a functioning whole. The parts or organs are connected in such a way that they form a larger whole, or organism, that can then function as an integrated mechanism. An alternative (and more complex) view of the body can conceive of it as being constituted by systems rather than organs. One may think of the immune system, the cardiovascular system, the nervous system, and so on. These systems are not located in specific places, they are not individual elements that can be put together. They are functional processes operating throughout the whole body. They are not literally body parts. Each system is "operationally closed." Blood circulation, for instance, can only be continued by further blood circulation. No other bodily system can take over this function. Nevertheless, in order for the blood circulation to go on, other systems in its environment, the immune system for instance, have to function simultaneously. When blood circulation stops, the immune system ceases to function, and when the immune system ceases to function, blood circulation stops. Within a complex system, such as the human body, there are a large number of subsystems that mutually provide the environment for one another. The relations between these systems are highly complex and constitute a wide variety of cutting lines (between the cardiovascular system and the immune system, between the nervous system and the cardiovascular system, between the immune system and the nervous system, etc.). The increased complexity of such a view of the functioning of the body can be demonstrated by the fact that each of these subsystems is more vital to the functioning of the overall system than any single organ. Organs can be replaced when they do not function well, but how does one replace the immune system or the nervous system?

In other words, first-order systems theory conceived of systems as "trivial machines" functioning on an input-output basis. A soda machine, for instance, could be conceived as a whole consisting of several mechanical parts. The functioning of the whole can then be externally steered by a specific input that mechanically and thus inevitably produces a certain output. By inserting a dollar and pressing a particular button, one causes the machine to eject a certain can. The steering of cars, or computers, or rockets, can be likewise explained on the basis of such a mechanistic cybernetics, in the sense of a "steering science."

Second-order cybernetics, on the contrary, focuses on how to deal with second-order systems, which are not conceived of as "trivial" but as "nontrivial" or "complex machines"—for example, a body essentially consisting not of organs, but of systems.[23] Because these systems are far

more complex, they are less predictable and cannot be easily steered.
There is no precisely predictable output when, for instance, one takes
a certain drug orally or puts CO_2 emissions into the air. There is not
even one singular event that could be identified as the "output" of such
an "input." The input of a drug will have various complex effects on the
various complex subsystem/environment relations within the body;
and the input of CO_2 into the air will have various complex effects on
the various complex subsystem/environment relations that constitute
the global climate.

Another decisive difference between first-order and second-order
systems theory has to do with their respective conceptions of change.
Strictly speaking, the change to which first-order systems may be
subject depends entirely on external factors—they are *allopoietic,* or
"externally generated." A soda machine may change from being full to
empty, or from being empty to full, depending on what people put into
it. It may also change from being not rusty to rusty depending on the
moisture it is exposed to. Second-order systems, do not change in such
a "creationist" way—in which all change is created from without, but in
an evolutionary way, where change is generated from *within.* Second-
order systems can therefore be conceived of as *autopoietic,* or "self-
generating." The evolution of species (within which the human species
is obviously both an input and an output) or the evolution of the climate (on which human activities have both input and are affected by
as an output) is not steered from the outside, but is self-steering. This
self-steering can hardly be called steering, though, since neither evolution nor climate change develop with a specific goal in mind. They are
not teleological. While the steering theory of first-order cybernetics is
concerned with how to steer systems by certain inputs so that a desired
output will be attained, second-order cybernetics assumes that no external steering is possible with respect to autopoietic second-order
systems such as, for instance, the climate of the earth, biological organisms, minds, or, for Luhmann, *society.* For all these systems, input is
also output and vice versa. In other words, input and output are interconnected through feedback loops. Autopoietic systems are immanent
systems—with their inside out and their outside in.[24]

As a systems theorist, Luhmann was not a traditional Cartesian dualist proposing the coexistence of two fundamental substances such as *res cogitans* and *res extensa,* or mind and body. He was rather a "triadist," assuming that there are at least three different kinds of autopoietic systems—and perhaps many more.[25] These systems are distinct because they operate in different ways. Biological systems, such as bodies, operate through life processes such as blood circulation, nervous activity, digestion, reproduction, and the division of cells. Mental systems operate through mental operations such as thoughts, feelings, and emotions. Luhmann saw himself as a sociologist and therefore focused primarily on a third kind of system that neither digests nor thinks, namely social systems. These systems *communicate.* Just as a second-order systemic biologist would want to describe the functioning of the various subsystems within a body and their effects on one another, Luhmann intended to describe the functioning and mutual couplings of the various communication systems in society. For instance, there is the economic system, where money and financial values circulate; the political system, where power is generated and perpetuated; the legal system, which operates on the basis of establishing distinctions between what is legal and what is not. Just as the human body has, via "emergence," evolved and developed all kinds of various function systems within itself, society has also evolved and brought forth a number of improbable (given the unlimited range of what had been evolutionarily possible) ways of operating through communication. Therefore, society basically consists of the various types of communication that more or less coincidentally or contingently emerged through processes of social evolution. Social "life" (metaphorically speaking—because society does not live, only bodies do) takes place in the form of legal, political, economic, intimate, educational, scientific, religious, medical communication, and so on. All of these types of communication emerged as autopoietic communication systems functioning within society. Within society, they are all environments for one another.

What is more, society and communication systems have evolved within the extrasocial environment of minds and bodies, or mental and biological systems. Without bodies and minds in the environment of society, there would be no communication, just as there would be no fish without water. However, in the same way that one should not confuse the fish with the water, one should not confuse society or communication systems with "people." That human beings think and live is a necessary environmental condition for any communication system to evolve. If nobody lives or thinks, then there cannot be any society. Nevertheless, human life and human thoughts and feelings are not communicative operations; they function outside of society. "Only communication can communicate,"[26] and not humans. This is probably the most radical communication-theoretical statement resulting from Luhmann's social systems theory.

Theory of Communication

Luhmann's self-declared "radically antihumanist" theory of society is, also a radically antihumanist theory of communication.[27] To repeat: this does not deny that there cannot be human communication without human thought and human life; it only confirms this commonsense assumption. Nor does it mean that Luhmann has anything against humans or their bodies or minds, only that he thinks that humanist—or, perhaps better, anthropological—concepts are unfit to theoretically describe and analyze communication. Luhmann supposes that communication, biological processes, and mental processes are operationally closed for one another. While they need one another in their environment in order to exist—and this mutual existential dependency Luhmann calls (borrowing once more from Maturana and Varela) "structural coupling"—their operations have no "connectivity": blood circulation cannot be continued by thinking about blood circulation—the blood actually has to move. Similarly, one cannot pass an exam by simply having all the right answers in mind. One actually has to write something down. Only what is written down can be checked by the instructor, not the thoughts one had while writing. And, the grade never (often fortunately for both instructor and student) shows what the instructor actually thought or felt when reading the exam. An exam is a communicative product that cannot and does not express all of the mental activities (not to mention the bodily processes) that were going on in the person who wrote it. A grade does not express, in any psychologically significant way, anything that was going on in the instructor's thoughts. Otherwise, all instructors assigning a grade of 80 must have similar or identical thoughts when assigning it.

Luhmann's theory aims at replacing any kind of mental or humanist definition of communication with a purely functional one. He strictly avoids speaking of communication in terms of "expression," "exchange," or "agency." There are no senders or receivers, and nothing is transmitted—at least not mentally or physically. Transferring money from your account to mine is a financial transaction between accounts that are "addressed" to the two of us, but nothing is "exchanged" or "transmitted" from your mind or body to mine in this case. The same is true, according to Luhmann for *all* communication. Even the most intimate lovers cannot literally exchange their ideas or feelings. Eva Knodt describes the "hermeneutic despair" arising from this impossibility quite impressively in her foreword to *Social Systems:* "In the opening scene of *Danton's Death,* the nineteenth-century German playwright Georg Büchner dramatizes what is easily recognized as the primal scene of hermeneutic despair. In response to his lover's attempt to reassure herself of the bond of understanding between them, the protagonist makes a silent gesture toward her forehead and then replies: "—there, there, what lies behind this? Go on, we have crude senses. To understand one another? We would have to break open each other's skulls and pull the thoughts out of the fibres of our brains."[28] But, of course, thoughts are not to be found (fortunately, one might add) in brain fibers either. Brains, minds, and (even intimate) communication are operationally closed to one another. There are no thoughts or feelings in the brain or in communication. They remain operations of mental systems. (Interestingly enough, it can be concluded that the common contemporary assumption that thoughts and feelings are located in the brain is thus as unwarranted as the ancient Greek and Chinese assumptions that the heart is the organ of mental activity.)

Instead of a cognitive or humanist model of exchange or expression, Luhmann suggests a *functional* theory of communication. Communication cannot be adequately defined by including the environment of communication (humans, for example) in this definition. To define communication in terms of thoughts or ideas would be as misleading as defining mental processes in terms of brain physiology.

Luhmann thus suggests the following definition for communication: it is the functional synthesis of three moments or "selections," namely, announcement (*Mitteilung*),[29] information (*Information*), and understanding (*Verstehen*).

Language is, of course, one way of communicating. But there are many others too: signs, gestures, and media such as money or (examination) grades. In order for communication to work, all three selections have to come together. When I submit my grades to the registrar's office, I can expect that the announcement of this information is understood. I have never been to the registrar's office, and I do not know anybody there. I do not know what the people there look like or how they feel and think. And they do not know me. We have never talked to each other—not even exchanged personal emails. Nevertheless, our communication usually functions perfectly. When I fill in the grades on the spreadsheet, it is somehow understood "in" the registrar's office (and it does not at all matter by which exact human being) that the numbers are information on the student's grades that have been announced by the instructor of a specific class at the end of the term. Once more: yes, all sorts of mental and physical events need to happen in the environment of this communicative process in order for it to happen (students, instructors, and staff have to live and think), but from a functional perspective, the communication is operationally *not* independent but decoupled from these specific mental and physical operations. There is no exchange: the grades are not literally given from one person to another. And the "understanding" does not have to be correct. That many students often misunderstand me does not prevent my lectures from being held—rather the opposite. If they always immediately understood, there would not be much need for lectures. A failed exam based on a complete misunderstanding does not at all function less (as communication) than a good exam. They both allow for the assignment of a numerical grade, and they both contribute to the continuation of the education system.

Communication systems, and thus society, construct sense (*Sinn*). "Sense" here indicates the "horizon" (Luhmann borrows this term from Husserl) of the possible within which something gains a meaning. Assigning a grade of 80, for instance, has a meaning only insofar as it happens within a meaningful horizon of a grading scheme, a practice of issuing transcripts, the checking of such transcripts as a selection criterion for being hired or accepted into a graduate program, and so on. Communication systems (i.e., social systems) and mental systems are, according to Luhmann, "sense-processing systems" (*sinnverarbeitende Systeme*). They produce sense and then operate on the basis of having produced it. In the literal meaning of the expression, communication *makes sense,* that is, it *constructs* it.

The various communication systems within society all construct sense. As a "radical constructivist,"[30] Luhmann does not believe that society functions on the basis of any presocial universals. That something has an economic value, that something is perceived as a work of art, that some acts are considered legal and others not, that there is such a thing as political power, that there are religious institutions and beliefs—all of these are, according to Luhmann, various results of communicative construction. Unlike Socrates in the *Republic,* for instance, Luhmann does not believe that the "idea of justice" is a subject worthy of investigation. For him, to give just one example of his social constructivism, justice is a "contingency formula" (*Kontingenzformel*) that is produced within the legal system.[31] On the basis of this formula, the legal system can operate endlessly. It can declare things that were once neither legal nor illegal, smoking in houses, for instance, to become legal in some cases and illegal in others. These laws can be changed again in the future. At the same time, these operations in the legal system allow other systems in its environment to produce "resonance" in their own ways. The mass media, for instance, have new opportunities to construct scandalous news. It can be reported that a film star smoked a cigarette when being interviewed at a film festival—if not for the law's creative application of its contingency formula to smoking, this could not have constituted news on TV.

Biological systems have no specific evolutionary goal; they are geared toward procreation and proliferation. This is sometimes successful, sometimes not. Some species survive, others do not. Communication systems do not develop teleologically. The proliferation of legal communication and the legal system does not make society more just. The proliferation of political communication and the political system does not increasingly empower society. While communication systems do not progress, while we do not understand one another better and better, they do evolve by creating "connectivity." They develop mechanisms to continue their operations. One election allows for subsequent ones; today's news allow for tomorrow's; today's new bylaw allows for a new court case tomorrow.

Thus, despite not having any ultimate meaning, communication still makes sense; without leading to progress, communication still provides new opportunities; and without allowing us to understand one another completely, communication can still provide us with the illusion that we do: "indeed, understanding is practically always a misunderstanding without an understanding of the mis."[32]

Criticisms and Reactions

Luhmann's explicit "radical antihumanism" led, predictably, to a range of criticisms. Most of these can be traced back to the Frankfurt-Bielefeld controversy of the 1970s. While Luhmann's position and that of the Frankfurt school had too little in common to modify one another to any real extent, the debate led to clear formulations of the profound differences and incompatibilities. The Frankfurt school can be understood as attempting to follow Marx's famous dictum that philosophy—or theory of communication, in this case—should not only interpret the world, but also set out to change it.[33] The most basic difference between Habermas's and Luhmann's theory is a methodological one. Habermas intended to improve society by making it communicate more rationally, while Luhmann's theory was not only primarily descriptive, but tried to show the limitations of attempts at social steering. Given the high complexity of communication systems in contemporary society, he deemed such attempts as often being futile. King and Thornhill, in their study of Luhmann's theory on politics and law, have nicely summarized the ensuing criticisms of Luhmann that either came directly from authors of the Frankfurt school or were similar with respect to their line of attack. These criticisms can be easily modified to represent similar criticisms of Luhmann's theory of communication. A modified version of the various criticisms listed by King and Thornhill would accordingly accuse Luhmann with respect to

- his refusal to see communication as an instrument for progress in society,
- his failure to account for human agency in communication,
- the failure of his theoretical ideas to offer anything more than a new brand of conservatism,
- his rejection of rationality as a universal arbiter of the validity, value, and legitimacy of communication, and
- his reluctance to engage in debates over current political and social issues related to communication.[34]

Despite these foundational criticisms from ideologically inclined academics, Luhmann's theory had a significant impact on a wide range of disciplines in the humanities and social sciences.[35] This impact has so far, however, been mostly confined to Europe and Latin America. There has been a lively reception of his theory in Germany, Italy, England, Spain, and Spanish- and Portuguese-speaking countries outside of Europe. In North America, the reception of his theory has been rather limited. One may speculate on the reasons for this. I suggest that two of the reasons are the nonhumanist foundation of his theory of communication, which runs counter to the dominant discourses in North America that are founded on liberal or communitarian views on civil society, and the reader-unfriendly style of Luhmann's writings. Even though a good number of his works have been translated into English, and still more are forthcoming, the often cryptic and convoluted writing style does not appeal to North American readers.[36]

Despite North American academia's reluctance to study Luhmann's theory, it may well become increasingly relevant, perhaps particularly because the nonhumanist aspects of communication highlighted by Luhmann are especially obvious in this part of the world. Recent developments in the economy, the mass media, and politics cry out, at least in my view, for analytic descriptions that go beyond, for instance, explanations of a phenomenon such as the economic crisis that emerged in 2008 in such simplistic humanist terms as "greed." Perhaps the following quote may be representative of the future reception of Luhmann's work in North American communication studies: "Communications, and signalling more generally, are aspects of social structure/process rather than a matter of independent cognitions. All this reasoning was pioneered by Luhmann."[37]

ABBREVIATIONS

Listed below are abbreviations for the works cited most frequently in this study. Niklas Luhmann is the sole author unless otherwise noted.

Barbarism | "Beyond Barbarism." In Hans-Georg Moeller, *Luhmann Explained: From Souls to Systems*. Chicago: Open Court, 2006. 261–272.

Chirurg | "Chirurg auf der Parkbank: Des Wählers Freiheit, eine Illusion." *Frankfurter Allgemeine Zeitung* (June 9, 1994): 35.

Cognition | "Cognition as Construction." In Hans-Georg Moeller, *Luhmann Explained: From Souls to Systems*. Chicago: Open Court, 2006. 241–260.

Deconstruction | "Deconstruction as Second-Order Observing." *New Literary History* 24 (1993): 763–782.

EC | *Ecological Communication*. Trans. John Bednarz Jr. Chicago: University of Chicago Press, 1989.

EI | *Einführung in die Systemtheorie*. Heidelberg: Carl-Auer-Systeme, 2002.

ES | *Essays on Self-Reference*. New York: Columbia University Press, 1990.

Fussball | "Der Fußball." *Frankfurter Allgemeine Zeitung* 152 (July 4, 1990): N3.

Gerechtigkeit | "Gerechtigkeit in den Rechtssystemen der modernen Gesellschaft." *Rechtstheorie* 4 (1973): 131–167.

GG | *Die Gesellschaft der Gesellschaft*. Frankfurt/Main: Suhrkamp, 1997.

GI | *Grundrechte als Institution: Ein Beitrag zur politischen Soziologie*. Berlin: Duncker and Humblot, 1965.

Globalization | "Globalization or World Society? How to Conceive of

Modern Society?" *International Review of Sociology* 7, no. 1 (March 1997): 67–79.

Kapitalismus   "Kapitalismus und Utopie." *Merkur* 48 (1994): 189–198.

KG   *Die Kunst der Gesellschaft.* Frankfurt/Main: Suhrkamp, 1997. Trans. Eva Knodt as *Art as a Social System.* Stanford: Stanford University Press, 2000.

Limits   "Limits of Steering." *Theory, Culture, and Society* 14, no. 1 (1997): 41–57.

LS   *Law as a Social System.* Trans. Klaus A. Ziegert. Oxford: Oxford University Press, 2005. 468.

Meinung   "Meinungsfreiheit, öffentliche Meinung, Demokratie." In *Meinungsfreiheit als Menschenrecht,* ed. Ernst-Joachim Lampe. Baden-Baden: Nomos, 1998. 99–110.

Mind   "How Can the Mind Participate in Communication?" In *Materialities of Communication,* ed. H. U. Gumbrecht and K. L. Pfeiffer. Stanford: Stanford University Press, 1994.

N   *Gibt es in unserer Gesellschaft noch unverzichtbare Normen?* Heidelberg: C. F. Müller Juristischer Verlag, 1993.

OM   *Observations on Modernity.* Trans. William Whobrey. Stanford: Stanford University Press, 1998.

P   *Protest.* Frankfurt/Main: Suhrkamp,1996.

Paradox   "Das Paradox der Menschenrechte und drei Formen seiner Entfaltung." In *Soziologische Aufklärung.* Vol. 6. Opladen: Westdeutscher Verlag, 1995.

Parteien   "Die Unbeliebtheit der politischen Parteien." In *Politik ohne Projekt? Nachdenken über Deutschland,* ed. Siegfried Unseld. Frankfurt/Main: Suhrkamp, 1993. 43–53.

PG   *Die Politik der Gesellschaft.* Frankfurt: Suhrkamp, 2002.

Postmodern   "Why Does Society Describe Itself as Postmodern?" *Cultural Critique* 30 (1995): 171–186.

PR   Niklas Luhmann and Karl-Eberhard Schorr. *Problems of Reflection in the System of Education.* Trans. Rebecca A. Neuwirth. New York: Waxman, 2000.

R   *Risk: A Sociological Theory.* Trans. Rhodes Barrett. New York: De Gruyter, 1993.

RM	*The Reality of the Mass Media.* Trans. Kathleen Cross. Stanford: Stanford University Press, 2000.
SA	*Soziologische Aufklärung.* Vol. 6. Opladen: Westdeutscher Verlag, 1995.
SC	*Short Cuts.* Frankfurt/Main.: Zweitausendeins. 2000.
Semantik	"Staat und Politik: Zur Semantik der Selbstbeschreibung politischer Systeme." In *Soziologische Aufklärung 4. Beiträge zur funktionalen Differenzierung der Gesellschaft.* Opladen: Westdeutscher Verlag, 1987. 74–103.
SS	*Social Systems.* Trans. John Bednarz Jr. with Dirk Baecker. Stanford: Stanford University Press, 1995.
Systemreferenz	"Die Systemreferenz von Gerechtigkeit: Erwiderung auf die Ausführungen von Ralf Dreier." *Rechtstheorie* 5 (1974): 201–203.
TG	Niklas Luhmann and Jürgen Habermas. *Theorie der Gesellschaft oder Sozialtechnolgie: Was leistet die Systemforschung?* Frankfurt/Main.: Suhrkamp, 1971.
Wahl	"Wie haben wir gewählt? Aber haben wir wirklich gewählt—oder hat das Volk gewürfelt?" *Frankfurter Allgemeine Zeitung* no. 246 (Oct. 22, 1994): 29.
WG	*Die Wissenschaft der Gesellschaft.* Frankfurt/Main: Suhrkamp, 1990.
World Society	"The World Society as a Social System." *Essays on Self-Reference.* New York: Columbia University Press, 1990. 175–188.
WP	*Die neuzeitlichen Wissenschaften und die Phänomenologie.* Vienna: Picus, 1996.

NOTES

Preface

1. See Globalization. An excellent systems-theoretical analysis of the financial crisis is Elena Esposito, *The Future of Futures* (Cheltenham: Edgar Elgar, forthcoming).

2. Globalization 69, 77, 74.

3. Ibid., 74. Luhmann continues: "And then, the calamity is no longer exploitation and suppression, but neglect. This society makes very specific distinctions with respect to its environment, for example, usable and not usable resources with respect to ecological questions or (excluded) bodies and (included) persons with respect to human individuals."

4. Michael King, "The Construction and Demolition of the Luhmann Heresy," *Law and Critique* 12 (2001): 1.

5. Globalization, 67, 72, 75.

6. Ibid., 76, 67.

7. Ibid., 76.

8. Ibid., 77.

1. The Trojan Horse

1. On the Anglophone reception of Luhmann's work, see Cary Wolfe, "Meaning as Event-Machine, or Systems theory and 'The Reconstruction of Deconstruction,'" in *Emergence and Embodiment: New Essays on Second-Order Systems Theory*, ed. Bruce Clarke and Mark B. N. Hansen (Durham: Duke University Press, 2009), 220–245. There are indications, however, that Luhmann's theory is becoming increasingly relevant in the United States, the UK, and Canada. In the United States, for instance, he is highly influential in posthumanist theory. See, for instance, N. Katherine Hayles, *How We Became Posthuman* (Chicago: University

of Chicago Press, 1999), and more recently, Bruce Clarke, *Posthuman Metamorphosis: Narrative and Systems* (New York: Fordham University Press, 2008), and Cary Wolfe, *What Is Posthumanism?* (Minneapolis: University of Minnesota Press, 2010).

2. Still more in the way of a sympathetic reception of Luhmann's theory is probably the theory itself. Not uncommonly, North American academics who actually make the painful effort to read and comprehend Luhmann are more appalled after this process than they were before it. Luhmann's fundamental opposition to and deconstruction of the basic consensus among the "liberal orthodoxy" that continues to strongly dominate North American social theory is too much to swallow for many of those who have been reared by and still flourish within it. Hardly any social theory contradicts the basic humanist assumptions underlying concepts of a "civil society," "liberty," "freedom," "democracy," and "justice" as thoroughly as Luhmann's. No wonder his impact on social theory in the United States and Canada is rather limited. Rodrigo Jokisch expresses a similar analysis of Luhmann's relatively insignificant success in North America in "Why Did Luhmann's Social Systems Theory Find So Little Resonance in the United States of America?" in *Addressing Modernity: Social Systems Theory and U.S. Culture,* ed. Hannes Bergthaller and Carsten Schinko (Amsterdam: Rodopi, 2011). This issue is discussed in more detail in chapter 3.

3. In P, 200. This volume was edited by Kai-Uwe Hellmann, who also conducted the interview that this quote is from. It was first published as "Systemtheorie und Protestbewegungen. Ein Interview." *Forschungsjournal Neue Soziale Bewegungen* 7, no. 2 (1994): 53–69.

4. In P, 74. This interview was originally published in the leftist German newspaper T*ageszeitung* on October 21, 1986, under the headline "Systemtheorie und Systemkritik, Ein Interview mit Heidi Renk und Marco Bruns."

5. I use the term "sublate" here as the common English translation for the Hegelian notion *Aufhebung.* It therefore has the threefold sense of "to lift to a higher level," "to negate and overcome," and "to preserve and maintain."

6. SS, 37; emphasis in the original.

2. Why He Wrote Such Bad Books

1. The review is by Herbert Gintis. See www.amazon.com/Luhmann-Explained-Souls-Systems-Ideas/dp/0812695984/ref=ntt_at_ep_dpi_3.

2. Asked about his writing habits, Luhmann stated: "When I have nothing else to do, I write the whole day; from 8.30 in the morning until noon. Then I take a short walk with my dog. Then I have some more time in the afternoon; from 2.00 to 4.00 pm. Then it is time for the dog again. . . . Well, and then I normally write in the evening until about 11.00 pm. . . . I have to say that I never force anything, I always do what I can do easily. I only write if I know immediately how to do it. When I come to a standstill for a moment, I put the thing aside and do something else." When asked by the interviewer what "else" he would do, Luhmann replied: "Well, I write other books. I always work on several books simultaneously" (SC, 29).

3. Ibid., 27.

4. Ibid., 26, 28.

5. There may soon be one book by Luhmann available in English that can be recommended as a first reading: an English translation of a posthumously published transcription of a lecture series by Luhmann titled *Introduction to Systems Theory* (*Einführung in die Systemtheorie*, Heidelberg: Carl-Auer-Systeme, 2002).

6. SS, 4.

7. Ibid., xxxvii.

3. The Fourth Insult

1. GG 35, 24. All translations, if not indicated otherwise, are mine.

2. Danilo Zolo, *Democracy and Complexity: A Realist Approach* (Oxford: Blackwell, 1992), ix.

3. Quoted in *Thomas Jefferson on Democracy*, ed. Saul K. Padover (New York: Penguin, 1946), 13.

4. On Luhmann and posthumanism, see Cary Wolfe, *What Is Posthumanism?* (Minneapolis: University of Minnesota Press, 2010), 249–263.

5. See, for instance, RM 3–4.

6. Jürgen Habermas, "Excursus on Luhmann's Appropriation of the Philosophy of the Subject through Systems Theory," in *The Philosophical Discourse of Modernity: Twelve Lectures*, translated by Frederick G.

Lawrence (Cambridge, Mass.: MIT Press, 1987). The quotation is on p. 372. One of the reviewers of my manuscript suggested that it might be more appropriate to change this term to "metabiotic" in order to avoid the mistaken impression that Luhmann shares the biological determinism of authors such as Richard Dawkins or E. O. Wilson. I fully agree with the reviewer that Luhmann is neither a biological determinist nor a social Darwinist. But, in my reading at least, this is not suggested by Habermas in the following quotation. Habermas simply points out that Luhmann's theory does not follow earlier mechanistic social theories but rather looks at society in a more organic and ecological way.

7. See chapter 5 for a more detailed discussion of this issue.

8. Mind, 371.

9. See chapter 8 for a more detailed discussion of this issue.

10. Limits, 49–50, 48.

11. OM, 35.

12. Limits, 47

13. Ibid., 48.

14. Ibid., 42.

15. Kapitalismus, 193–194.

16. John Gray, *Al Qaeda and What It Means to Be Modern* (New York: New Press, 2003), 47, 43.

17. Sigmund Freud, *Darstellungen der Psychoanalyse* (Frankfurt/Main: Fischer, 1969), 130–138.

18. Kapitalismus, 194.

19. Chirurg. See also Parteien, 44. In Parteien, Luhmann calls the concept of civil society a "sympathetic utopia."

20. Kapitalismus, 197.

21. PG, 113.

22. Ibid., 135. Technically speaking, democracy is based on a paradox of sovereignty. "Democracy means: the people themselves govern. And whom [do they govern]? The people of course" (PG 353). In a paradoxical fashion the people simultaneously give orders to themselves and obey themselves. Such self-descriptions remind Luhmann of theological conceptions but cannot be accepted as adequate analyses of the functioning of politics. Similar to the semantics of steering, the semantics of the people seems to be largely a symbolic power.

23. See Michael King and Chris Thornhill, *Niklas Luhmann's Theory of Politics and Law* (New York: Palgrave Macmillan. 2003), 204, for a summary of these criticisms.

24. See Limits.

25. On the boringness of contemporary philosophy with specific regard to ethics of the analytical variety, see Bernard Williams, *Morality: An Introduction to Ethics* (Cambridge: Cambridge University Press, 1993), xvii.

26. On the term "metacritical," see Günter Wohlfart, "Metacritique of Practical Reason," at www.guenter-wohlfart.de.

4. From Necessity to Contingency

1. Jürgen Habermas, *The Philosophical Discourse of Modernity: Twelve Lectures*, trans. Frederick Lawrence (Cambridge, Mass: MIT Press, 1987), 377; translation modified.

2. GG ,1097.

3. See Mikhail M. Bakhtin, *Literatur und Karneval* (Frankfurt/Main: Fischer, 1990), 49.

4. G. W. F. Hegel, *Phenomenology of Spirit*, trans. A. V. Miller (Oxford: Oxford University Press, 1977), 2. The German term *Wissenschaft* (which literally means something like "the creation of knowledge") encompasses all academic disciplines including natural sciences, social sciences, the humanities, and so on. See the more detailed discussion of this terminology later in this chapter.

5. See Geoffrey Winthrop-Young, "Silicon Sociology, or, Two Kings on Hegel's Throne? Kittler, Luhmann, and the Posthuman Merger of German Media Theory," *Yale Journal of Criticism* 13, no. 2 (2000): 391–420.

6. I am grateful to Günter Wohlfart for outlining in detail Hegel's indebtedness to Kant in private correspondence with me. Hegel, *Phenomenology*, 1, 14.

7. See Miller's spelling of "True" in his translation of the *Phenomenology*.

8. Ibid., 23–27, 56.

9. EI, 341.

10. See n6 above and Kant's *Critique of Pure Reason*, A 832/B860. See also Luhmann's appreciative remark on the "excessive, unsurpassable awareness of theory architecture that one finds in Kant or Hegel" in n19 in his

essay "Modernity in Contemporary Society" in OM, 116.

11. See GG, 11, and the appendix in this book.

12. P, 200.

13. Hegel, *Phenomenology*, 23.

14. Fussball.

15. See, for instance, Hegel, *Phenomenology*, 2.

16. Luhmann concludes his essay "Beyond Barbarism" with this statement: "If this diagnosis is only roughly correct, society can neither expect advice nor help from sociology. But it could make sense to search for theories that do more justice to the facts than the optimistic-critical traditional ways of thought within our discipline—justice to those facts with which society constructs itself" (Barbarism, 272).

17. Hegel, *Phenomenology*, 493.

18. GG, 1081.

19. Hegel, *Phenomenology*, 492.

20. Cognition, 250.

21. GG, 1122.

22. In *Social Systems*, Luhmann labels Hegel a "neo-humanist thinker," SS, 259.See also chapter 5 in this book.

23. WG.

24. See RM, 20.

25. See WG, 457.

26. See RM, 29.

27. In all these expressions the *genitivus subjectivus* and *genitivus objectivus* are used simultaneously. The title *The Science of Society,* for example, uses the word "society" in both an objective and subjective sense and thus means both the branch of science that has society as its object (i.e., "sociology" as the science that studies society) and refers to science as a general body of knowledge that is produced by society as the "subject" which "does" science (science as something that society engages in).

28. Hegel, *Phenomenology,* 45;WG, 10.

29. WG ,547.

30. Instead of *Roman* ("novel") one may therefore want to substitute, *Bildungsroman.*

31. OM, ix.

32. GG, 1097.

33. WP, 17.

34. WG, 159.

35. GG, 1097.

36. See RM, and the section on mass media in Hans-Georg Moeller, *Luhmann Explained: From Souls to Systems* (Chicago: Open Court, 2006), 119–161.

37. See SS, 5.

38. See also this interesting remark by Luhmann: "What we need after Hegel is a more pragmatic, more opportunistic, *more playful game-like approach to theory*" (Nico Stehr, "The Evolution of Meaning Systems: An Interview with Niklas Luhmann," *Theory, Culture, and Society* 1, no. 1 (1982): 33–48, here: 47; emphasis added). In his very brief introductory remark to a session at a conference on Hegel in 1977 Luhmann asked whether "ironical theories contain a higher potential of reflection" (Niklas Luhmann, "Zur Einführung," *Hegel-Studien*, Beiheft 17. Bonn: Bouvier, 1977, in *Ist Systematische Philosophie möglich?* Dieter Henrich, ed., 443–445; here: 445).

5. The Last Footnote to Plato

1. This has been remarkably different in certain non-Western discursive traditions such as the Chinese. In the Chinese tradition, a substantial mind-body division was never introduced. Quite to the contrary, the core philosophical vocabulary—which at the same time also constituted a core part of the "popular" vocabulary in practical fields such as medicine, politics, geomantics, and so on—contained several nondualistic notions such as *xin* (heart-mind), *qi* (energy), *dao* (way, truth), and many others that easily intertwined physical and intellectual connotations.

2. This is how Nietzsche argues in the section on the "four great errors" in *Twilight of the Idols*.

3. Rene Descartes, *The Passions of the Soul* (article 34, "How the soul and the body act on one another"). I am quoting from the translation by Elizabeth S. Haldane and G. R. T. Ross in *The Philosophical Works of Descartes* (Cambridge, UK: Cambridge University Press, 1970), 347.

4. An excellent brief summary of the history of cybernetics can be found in Bruce Clarke, *Posthuman Metamorphosis. Narrative and Systems* (New York: Fordham University Press, 2008), 4–7.

5. Luhmann speaks of a paradigm shift from the concept of part/whole dif-

ferences to system/environment differences: "Accordingly, a differentiated system is no longer simply composed of a certain number of parts and the relations among them; rather, it is composed of a relatively large number of operationally employable system/environment differences, which each, along different cutting lines, reconstruct the whole system as the unity of subsystem and environment" (SS 7).

6. See, for instance, GG, 117.

7. One may think here of James Lovelock's Gaia theory.

8. This is indirectly proved by Marxist or communist readings of Plato's most important text on social theory, namely the *Republic*.

9. SS, 9, 36.

10. SS, 36; RM, 66.

11. SS, 19.

12. See in particular section 4, part 1 in Hume's *An Inquiry Concerning Human Understanding* titled "Special Doubts Concerning the Operations of the Understanding."

6. Ecological Evolution

1. See for instance John Gray, *Straw Dogs: Thoughts on Humans and Other Animals* (London: Granta, 2002).

2. On Luhmann and Darwin, see Geoffrey Winthrop-Young, "On a Species of Origin: Luhmann's Darwin," *Configurations* 11 (2003): 305–349.

3. Jürgen Habermas, *The Philosophical Discourse of Modernity: Twelve Lectures,* trans. Frederick Lawrence (Cambridge, Mass.: MIT Press, 1987), 372. See chapter 3 in this book for a more detailed discussion of this term coined by Habermas.

4. SS, li.

5. See John Gray's deconstruction of this narrative in *Straw Dogs.*

6. On Luhmann's terminological discussion of history versus evolution, see "Evolution und Geschichte" in GG, 569–576.

7. The pun with *Wesen* and *gewesen* is not translatable into English. Literally, the sentence means: essence (*Wesen*) is what has been (*gewesen*).

8. Charles Darwin, *The Origin of Species* (Oxford: Oxford University Press, 1996), 51.

9. The most infamous example of equating biological evolutionary progress with social evolutionary progress is the Nazi ideology. See my comments

at the end of this chapter.

10. To my knowledge, Luhmann never uses the term "genealogy" as a component of his theoretical vocabulary.

11. See chapter 4 in this book.

12. For Luhmann's concept of sense, see the glossary entry in Hans-Georg Moeller, *Luhmann Explained: From Souls to Systems* (Chicago: Open Court, 2006), 225. Luhmann originally derived the concept from Husserl and defines it as a (contingent) actuality within a horizon of possibilities.

7. Constructivism as Postmodernist Realism

1. GG, 35.

2. A representative anthology of constructivist epistemology is *Die erfundene Wirklichkeit: Wie wissen wir, was wir zu wissen glauben? Beiträge zum Konstruktivismus,* ed. Paul Watzlawick (Munich: Piper, 1981). This volume includes essays by Paul Watzlawick, Ernst von Glasersfeld, Heinz von Foerster, Francisco Varela, and others. The explicit designation "radical constructivism" became academically popular in Germany (to my knowledge) through publications such as *Der Diskurs des radikalen Konstruktivismus,* ed. Siegfried J. Schmidt (Frankfurt/Main: Suhrkamp, 1987). It seems that Luhmann—as is obvious by his frequent citations— felt very much indebted to the earlier constructivists like von Glasersfeld, von Foerster, and Varela, but did not fully accept the later more "fashionable" constructivist developments as represented in the volume edited by S. J. Schmidt.

3. Cognition, 241. This essay may well be read as Luhmann's programmatic exposition of his version of radical (epistemological) constructivism.

4. SS, 2.

5. On "ontology," see GG, 893–912, in which Luhmann diagnoses a "complete breakdown of ontological metaphysics" in modern theory.

6. SS, 2.

7. See Wittgenstein's *Tractatus Logico Philosophicus,* 1: "Die Welt ist alles, was der Fall ist" (the world is everything that is the case; my translation), and 2: "Was der Fall ist, die Tatsache, ist das Bestehen von *Sachverhalten*" (what is the case—the actuality—is the existence of *facts* [my translation and my italics]).

8. See also chapter 4 in this book on the relation between Luhmann and

German idealism.

9. See Luhmann's clear rejection of Kant's "recantation" of a more radical constructivism in "Cognition as Construction," Hans-Georg Moeller, *Luhmann Explained: From Souls to Systems* (Chicago: Open Court, 2006), 241–260. Luhmann disapprovingly cites and annotates [in brackets], the following proposition from Kant's *Critique of Pure Reason*: "The mere, but empirically [!] determined consciousness of my own existence proves the existence of the objects [!] [and thus not only of something, N.L.] in the space [!] outside of myself," ("Cognition as Construction," 242n3).

10. As translated by G. H. R. Parkinson in Spinoza, *Ethics* (Oxford: Oxford University Press, 2000), 76.

11. GG, 35; LE, 239.

12. For an attempt to use this Luhmannian approach for an analysis of globalization, see Jean-Sebastien Guy, "The Name 'Globalization': Observing Society Observing Itself," in Ignacio Farias and Jose Ossandon, eds., *Observando Sistemas 2* (Mexico DF: Universidad Iberoamericana, forthcoming).

13. Cognition, 250.

14. RM, 6, 7 (emphasis added).

15. On Luhmann and Derrida, see Deconstruction.

16. SS, 498n19; italics in the original. Interestingly enough, following this statement, Luhmann refers approvingly to an article by Alfred Locker, "On the Ontological Foundations of the Theory of Systems," in *Unity Through Diversity: A Festschrift for Ludwig von Bertalanffy,* ed. William Gray and Nicholas D. Rizzo (New York: 1973), 1:537–572. At least indirectly, Luhmann thus accepts an ontological dimension of his theory.

17. Jean Clam, *Was heißt, sich an Differenz statt an Identität orientieren? Zur De-ontologisierung in Philosophie und Sozialwissenschaft* (Konstanz: UVK, 2002). As the subtitle says, Clam perceives the shift from identity to difference as "de-ontologization." I like to conceive of the shift as one from "classical" ontologies to "postmodernist" ones.

18. Ray Monk, *Ludwig Wittgenstein: The Duty of Genius* (London: Penguin, 1990), 536–537. As the source for the account of the conversation between Drury and Wittgenstein, Monk refers to *Recollections of Wittgenstein,* ed. Rush Rhees (Oxford: 1984), 157.

19. "European Rationality," in OM, 23.

20. Ibid., 35.

21. Donald Phillip Verene has an excellent essay (included in an altogether excellent book) titled "The Topsy-turvy World," in Verene, *Hegel's Recollection: A Study of Images in the* Phenomenology of Spirit (Albany: SUNY Press, 1985), 39–58.

22. According to Verene, Hegel's *"Phenomenology* can be seen as a philosophical ship of fools, in which each stage is a different compartment in the ship, and the individual reader, following the original course of the illusions of consciousness itself, works his way toward wisdom" (*Hegel's Recollection*, 54).

23. In the preface to Wittgenstein, *Philosophical Investigations*.

24. The original German expression he uses is "Zurück auf den rauhen Boden!" (*Philosophical Investigations*, 107).

25. Ibid., 107.

8. Democracy as a Utopia

1. This expression is used by Edwin Czerwick in his *Systemtheorie der Demokratie: Begriffe und Strukturen im Werk Luhmanns* (Wiesbaden: Verlag für Sozialwissenschaften, 2008), 134.

2. In private conversation, Jason Dockstader suggested that the fact that these decisions have to be made, and that they are often not made by the political system, indicates that there exists one social system Luhmann never wrote about, namely the war or military system.

3. RM, 50.

4. Semantik, 80. See also Czerwick, *Systemtheorie der Demokratie,* 65.

5. Wahl.

6. Czerwick, *Systemtheorie der Demokratie,* 98. Czerwick (and Luhmann) obviously have European democracies in mind with this description. In the United States, the government and the president are not elected by Parliament, but by a different political body—which, however, is also elected, so that the "circles" are basically the same in Europe and the United States.

7. PG ,366.

8. PG 366, 283.

9. Parteien, 52.

10. Meinung, 107. With respect to the notion of "symbolic rule" Luhmann refers in a footnote to the following literature, Thurman W. Arnold, *The Symbols of Government* (New Haven: Yale University Press, 1935); Murray Edelman, *The Symbolic Uses of Politics* (Urbana: University of Illinois Press,1967); Marcelo Neves, *A Constitucionalização Symbólica* (Sao Paolo, 1994).

11. Michael King and Chris Thornhill, *Niklas Luhmann's Theory of Politics and Law* (New York: Palgrave MacMillan, 2003), 203–225. See the appendix for further details on King's and Thornhill's analysis.

12. Czerwick, 191–192. I think Czerwick's book is overall an excellent and highly accurate study of Luhmann's concept of democracy.

9. Conclusion

1. My friend's name is Jari Grosse-Ruyken.

2. One example is John Mingers, "Can Social Systems be Autopoietic? Assessing Luhmann's Social Theory," *Sociological Review* 50 (2002): 278–299.

3. In the following, I use the term "theory" in reference to Luhmann's conception of (super)theory.

4. See Michael King and Anton Schutz, "The Ambitious Modesty of Niklas Luhmann," *Journal of Law and Society* 21 (1994): 261–287.

5. I hope the ironical nature of this sentence may not be noticed only by readers who look at this note.

6. See chapter 4.

7. How modern science does not simply "grow" by accumulating knowledge but functions rather differently has most prominently been outlined in the works of Thomas Kuhn.

8. Translation by Cyril Smith at www.marxists.org/archive/marx/works/1845/theses/index.htm.

9. See the discussion of the grammatically ambiguous titles of many of Luhmann's books (e.g., *Die Gesellschaft der Gesellschaft* [The Society of Society]) in chapter 4.

10. *Apology*, 38a.

11. Gilles Deleuze, *Logique du sens* (Paris: Les Éditions de Minuit: 1969).

12. See his *Die neuzeitlichen Wissenschaften und die Phänomenologie* (Vienna: Picus, 1996), 45–46.

13. See the discussion of this sentence in chapter 4.

14. For Luhmann on morality and ethics, see "Paradigm Lost: On the Ethical Reflection of Morality: Speech on the Occasion of the Award of the Hegel Prize, 1989," *Thesis Eleven* 29 (1991): 82–94; "The Code of the Moral," *Cardozo Law Review* 14 (1992–93): 995–1009; "The Sociology of the Moral and Ethics," *International Sociology* 11 (1996): 27–36; "The Morality of Risk and the Risk of Morality," *International Review of Sociology* 3 (1987): 87–101. See also the section on negative ethics in my *Luhmann Explained: From Souls to Systems* (Chicago: Open Court: 2006), 108–114.

15. If readers now begin to wonder if there is a difference between social systems theory and postmodernism, here's what Luhmann says: "Is this, after all, a postmodern theory? Maybe, but then the adherents of postmodern conceptions will finally know what they are talking about" ("Why Does Society Describe Itself as Postmodern?" *Cultural Critique* [Spring 1995]: 171–186; here, 184).

16. Barbarism, 269.

17. World Society, 187.

18. Ludwig Wittgenstein, "Lecture on Ethics," *Philosophical Review* 74, no. 1 (1965): 3–12.

Appendix

1. Quoted from an interview with Luhmann by Wolfgang Hagen for Radio Bremen; broadcast on October 2, 1997. The transcript is at www.radio-bremen.de/online/luhmann/es_gibt_keine_biographie.pdf. The translation is mine. In German, Luhmann uses the term "Nazi-Umwelt" in analogy to the "System-Umwelt" terminology of his theory. Unless noted otherwise, all biographical information presented in the appendix is taken from Luhmann's statements in this interview.

2. Drinking beer at a public festivity while mingling with the local population is considered a social virtue in Germany. Those who refrain from such activities may encounter difficulties in obtaining a position as a civil servant.

3. A comprehensive bibliography of Luhmann's writings is Sylke Schiermeyer and Johannes F. K. Schmidt, "Niklas Luhmann—Schriftenverzeichnis," *Soziale Systeme: Zeitschrift für soziologische Theorie* 4, no. 1 (1988): 233–263.

4. See www.radiobremen.de/online/luhmann/es_gibt_keine_biographie. pdf.

5. GG, 11.

6. SS, 4.

7. TG.

8. P, 71.

9. On the difference between first- and second-order cybernetics, see Bruce Clarke, *Posthuman Metamorphosis: Narrative and Systems* (New York: Fordham University Press, 2008), 4–7.

10. SC, 25.

11. See the chapter on Luhmann in Jürgen Habermas, *The Philosophical Discourse of Modernity: Twelve Lectures* (Cambridge, Mass.: MIT Press, 1987).

12. All books except the last one were published by Suhrkamp (Frankfurt/ Main); *Die Realität der Massenmedien* (Opladen: Westdeutscher Verlag). *Das Recht der Gesellschaft,* trans. Klaus A. Ziegart (Oxford: Oxford University Press, 2002); *Die Kunst der Gesellschaft,* trans. Eva Knodt (Stanford: Stanford University Press, 2000); *Die Realität der Massenmedien,* trans. Kathleen Cross (Stanford: Stanford University Press, 1996).

13. *Die Religion der Gesellschaft* (The Religion of Society) (Frankfurt/ Main: Suhrkamp, 2000); *Die Politik der Gesellschaft* (The Politics of Society) (Frankfurt/Main: Suhrkamp, 2000); *Das Erziehungssystem der Gesellschaft* (The Education System of Society) (Frankfurt/Main: Suhrkamp, 2002).

14. Published by Suhrkamp (Frankfurt/Main); an English translation is currently being prepared.

15. Published by Suhrkamp (Frankfurt/Main). The translation is by Jeremy Gaines and Doris L. Jones, *Love as Passion: The Codification of Intimacy* (Cambridge, UK: Polity Press, 1986). A number of Luhmann's articles on semantics were published in four volumes by Suhrkamp (Frankfurt/Main) under the title *Gesellschaftsstruktur und Semantik* (Social Structure and Semantics) in 1980, 1981, 1989, and 1995.

16. The translation is by John Bednarz Jr. (Chicago: University of Chicago Press, 1989).

17. The translation is by Rhodes Barrett (New York: De Gruyter, 1993).

18. Deconstruction.

19. Postmodern, 179.

20. For a more detailed introduction to Luhmann's theory see my book *Luhmann Explained: From Souls to Systems* (Chicago: Open Court, 2006).

21. On second-order systems theory, see Clarke, *Posthuman Metamorphosis*, 7;on second-order cybernetics and second-order emergence, see N. Katherine Hayles, *How We Became Posthuman* (Chicago: University of Chicago Press, 1999), 6, 243.

22. SS, 7.

23. The terminological distinction between trivial and nontrivial machines goes back to Heinz von Foerster. See Clarke, *Posthuman Metamorphosis*, 141–142.

24. I borrow this citation of a Beatles song from an essay by Ranulph Glanville and Francisco Varela, "Your Inside Is Out and Your Outside Is In (Beatles 1968)," in *Applied Systems and Cybernetics,* vol. 2, ed. George E. Lasker (Oxford: Pergamon, 1981), 638–641.

25. See chapter 5.

26. See Mind.

27. GG, 35.

28. SS, xxiv.

29. This term has also been translated into English as "utterance."

30. SS, xxiv.

31. See LS.

32. RM, 97.

33. As formulated in the eleventh thesis against Feuerbach.

34. See Michael King and Chris Thornhill, *Niklas Luhmann's Theory of Politics and Law* (New York: Palgrave Macmillan. 2003), 204.

35. For an overview of Luhmann's academic impact in Germany and Europe, see Henk de Berg and Johannes Schmidt, eds., *Rezeption und Reflexion: Zur Resonanz der Systemtheorie Niklas Luhmanns außerhalb der Soziologie* (Suhrkamp: Frankfurt/Main, 2000).

36. See chapter 2.

37. Harrison C. White, *Identity and Control: How Social Formations Emerge,* 2nd ed. (Princeton: Princeton University Press, 2008), 337.

INDEX